Saints in Arms

AMS PRESS
NEW YORK

STANFORD UNIVERSITY PUBLICATIONS
UNIVERSITY SERIES

HISTORY, ECONOMICS, AND POLITICAL SCIENCE
VOLUME XVIII

Saints in Arms

PURITANISM AND DEMOCRACY

IN CROMWELL'S ARMY

LEO F. SOLT

STANFORD UNIVERSITY PRESS
STANFORD, CALIFORNIA
LONDON: OXFORD UNIVERSITY PRESS
1959

International Standard Book Number: 0-404-50976-2

Library of Congress Catalog Card Number: 74-153355

AMS PRESS INC.
NEW YORK, N.Y. 10003

To

MARY ELLEN

———

Preface

My interest in Puritan theology and politics began at the State University of Iowa under the tutelage of George L. Mosse and Goldwin Smith and was continued at Columbia University under William Haller and Garrett Mattingly. I am indebted to these men for invaluable guidance in the early stages of my work. I wish also to thank Horton Davies of Princeton University and Maurice Ashley, editor of *The Listener,* for their helpful suggestions after having read my manuscript. The criticism of my junior colleagues in the Department of History at Indiana University as well as that of my former colleague at the University of Massachusetts, Robert M. Kingdon, has been of inestimable help in the late stages of this book. I am also indebted to the librarians of the British Museum for access to the Thomason collection and to the librarians, particularly Mrs. Sue Foster, of Union Theological Seminary for access to the McAlpin collection. Portions of this book have been published in articles in *Church History, The Church Quarterly Review, The Journal of Ecclesiastical History,* and *The Listener,* and will be published in the *Archiv für Reformationgeschichte.*

L. F. S.

Bloomington, Indiana
April 1959

Contents

Saints in Arms

———————

Introduction

Many scholars in recent years, in both the United States and England, have concerned themselves with the contributions of the Puritan Revolution to the growth of democratic thought.[1] Starting with the Leveller speeches around the campfires of Cromwell's New Model Army in the summer and fall of 1647, which contain some of the most eloquent and perceptive remarks ever made about the nature of the democratic process, there has been a tendency to ascribe the political and religious ideas set forth there as characteristic of the whole Puritan movement, or more particularly, of all of the soldiers of the New Model Army. This is the interpretation that has prevailed for the last three decades, and there is some good evidence, one must admit, to support it.

Unfortunately, however, these same speeches have given rise to considerable theorizing about the link between Puritanism and democracy which must, in the light of present-day research, be suspect. Only a few recent writers have argued that Puritanism has authoritarian implications as well.[2] It is the purpose of this volume to reexamine the prevailing interpretation in the light of the press and pulpit polemics of the saints in arms—the chaplains of the New Model Army. These chaplains were the official emissaries for the spiritual, and sometimes political, edification of the troops. From this reexamination I hope to put the theme of Puritanism and democracy in a more proper historical perspective.

[1]Superscript numbers refer to Notes, pp. 105–22.

I have chosen this testing ground not because I think the New Model's chaplains were necessarily typical Puritans (although they were representative of a certain kind of Puritanism which was close to the main stream), but because no other institution or group of people, ironically, has been regarded as the nursery school for so many radical ideas in the seventeenth century. The basic argument at Putney, as indeed throughout the entire century, was whether government should be by good men or by good laws, whether by grace or by nature. Or to put it another way, the relation of political thought to religious thought in the Puritan Revolution turns on the question of why some groups were led to claim the privileges and rule of the saints based upon God's Free Grace, whereas others preached the equality and sovereignty of the people based upon natural law. Those in the first category upheld the righteousness of good and religious men to rule over the evil and irreligious; it was their authoritarian influence, for example, that led to the calling of the Nominated or Barebones Parliament. The others upheld the natural rights of all the people as interpreted by their representatives freely chosen for Parliament; this was the democratic idea behind the program of the Levellers.

We may begin by stating briefly the case that has been made by scholars for the prevailing interpretation.[3] Their work tends to play up the first member of each of the following pairs of politico-religious polarities: (1) liberty and authority, (2) unity and uniformity, (3) separatism and millenarianism, (4) equality and sainthood, (5) covenant and grace, (6) elective polity and anarchy, (7) fundamental law and power, (8) mixed government and policy, and (9) masses and classes. Parenthetically, any case for an authoritarian strain in Puritanism will have to be found in the second part of the same pairs of polarities.

Liberty is achieved by appealing to a source of authority—divine grace—from which a believer may defy the authorities of this world. The inward unity of God's revealed truth, as opposed to the external uniformity of some magistrate, is made known to the conscience of the true believer, and in case of conflict within the human conscience, resort is made to free debate and discussion. The complete separation of grace and nature—the church and the state—tends to work against a millenarian eschatology, i.e., rule by the saints, and ideally provides for religious toleration for all. From a presumed correspondence between grace and nature come three additional concepts: equality, covenant, and elective polity. Equality suggests that as all believers have an equal claim to the favor of God, so do all individuals have an equal claim to the favor of the civil magistrate. Covenant suggests that a bilateral agreement on mutual rights and obligations is characteristic of both the relation between the believer and God and the relation between the believer and his fellow men. Two additional concepts, fundamental law and mixed government, stand in opposition to millenarian eschatology. Fundamental law limits the absolute power of God transposed to an absolute secular power, e.g., the New Model Army. Mixed government or a separation of powers limits the notion of policy or *raison d'état* in which divinity is asked to perform Machiavellian tricks. The masses are usually the poor and oppressed members of society who are the recipients of social amelioration, in this instance as a result of an attack upon the professional classes: the clergy, the lawyers, and the university professors.

Of the above-listed pairs of politico-religious polarities, (1) and (2) will be treated in chapter three, (3) in chapters four and five, (4), (5), and (6) in chapter four, (7) and (8) in chapter five, and (9) in chapter six. Chapters one and two present the necessary historical and theological background. Inasmuch as the chaplains' fundamental theological ideas, so important to an understanding of their political ideas, were an outgrowth of their experiences in the New Model Army, I have thought it best to start with a narrative of their activities from the time of their entrance into the army of saints in 1644 and 1645 until the departure of most of them at the end of 1647 and the beginning of 1648.

The Case of the Army Stated

When Richard Baxter visited the New Model Army after the battle of Naseby, he found the majority of the soldiers and many of the officers to be what he called "honest, sober, Orthodox men." However, to his great distress there were also "a few proud, self-conceited, hot-headed Sectaries," who quickly became Oliver Cromwell's favorites. He hastily added that the "Sectaries" were only about one in twenty, but he had to admit that they were the "soul of the Army," and by their "very heat and activity" bore the rest along with them. These "Sectaries," according to Baxter, held vehement disputes in favor of liberty of conscience, "that is, that the Civil magistrate had nothing to do to determine of any thing in matters of Religion, by constraint or restraint, but every man might not only *hold,* but *preach* and *do* in matters of Religion what he pleased."[1] Liberty of conscience was also a basic tenet of that religious group known as the Independents.[2] It seems clear that this was the quality that Cromwell had in mind when he said that he desired only those men in the Army who were of an "independent judgment."[3] Whether they were called sectaries or Independents, Cromwell's Army favorites found coherence as a group chiefly in their opposition to the Presbyterian form of church government. Even Edward Hyde, later Earl of Clarendon, from his island retreat at Jersey, had not failed to notice that Cromwell and his officers admitted no chaplains into the Army except those who inveighed against the Presbyterian form of church government for being more tyrannical than Episcopacy had been.[4]

Prior to the reorganization of the Parliamentary Army in accordance with the New Model Ordinance of 17 February 1645, the chaplains for the Army's regiments had been largely Presbyterians. It is customary to say that with the new-modeling of the Parliamentary forces by Cromwell, the Presbyterians left and the New Model Army took on a definitely Independent outlook. However, a word of caution ought to be given regarding the use of the term "Independent." They were Independents in what George Yule has called the "radical" sense, i.e., in their advocacy of religious toleration and experiential religion; but not in the more "orthodox" sense—i.e., they did not subscribe to either the ecclesiastical or the theological views of the Congregational "Dissenting Brethren."[5] For example, the "Dissenting Brethren" of the Westminster Assembly of Divines, although close to the Presbyterians in the Federal Covenant theology,[6] advocated a "gathered church" principle which stressed the independent autonomy of the local congregation as opposed to the hierarchical control of the Presbyterian classis, synod, and assembly.

Now it is true that Baxter had been invited by Cromwell at an earlier date at Cambridge to form the "Ironsides" into a gathered church (he refused, much to his regret later). Nevertheless, the new chaplains of the Army were inclined, for the most part, to set aside church forms altogether—be they Presbyterian, Congregational, or whatever—and the rest of the Army, especially after its new-modeling, felt the same way. Baxter, prompted by a sense of belated urgency, joined Colonel Whalley's regiment as a chaplain before Goring's rout in the west in order to counteract the new religious spirit within the Army. Now, however, he was spurned by Cromwell. For a year and a half Baxter made it his daily self-appointed task to root out by discourse the soldiers' "mistakes," both religious and political.[7]

Among the "mistakes" that Baxter observed in the New Model, in addition to liberty of conscience, were the soldiers' statements "sometimes for State Democracy, and sometimes for Church Democracy . . . sometimes about Free-grace and Free-will, and all the Points of Antinomianism and Arminianism." In other words, in Baxter's mind, those men who were attacking Federal Covenant theology by upholding its logical extremes were the very same men who were demanding additional political liberties as well as liberty of conscience. It is certainly true that William Dell and John Saltmarsh, whom Baxter called the "two great preachers at the Head Quarters" of the Army, believed in the theological doctrine of "justification by free-grace," and were therefore often identified by their enemies as Antinomians. Also, an anonymous letter writer reported to Thomas Edwards, author of *Gangraena,* that both Dell and Salt-marsh "pressed hard to have the law of Love and Liberty observed, that there may be an equality; that is their phrase and the Anabaptists." As for Cromwell, Baxter stated that the Lieu-tenant-General did "not openly profess what Opinion he was of himself; But the most that he said for any was for *Anabaptism* and *Antinomianism,* which he usually seemed to own." More dangerous than all the rest, according to Baxter, was one group which followed the "Jesuitical way" of free will and opposed all government but "popular" government. This was the group which later became known as the Levellers. Faced with such a formidable opposition as this, and sorely afflicted by an illness which nearly took his life, Baxter assumed that the will of God was against his efforts and departed from the Army.[8]

Baxter's Army experiences point directly to our basic problem in this study. They also raise some questions for which answers will be sought in the remainder of this chapter, to wit: Who were these sectaries—these "prodigious new blazing stars" —and what were their duties in the New Model? Just how "godly" was the New Model? And finally, what role did the Army preachers play in the dramatic politico-religious debate that split the New Model Army in the fall of 1647?

SOME PRODIGIOUS NEW BLAZING STARS

Dell, Saltmarsh, and Hugh Peters were the three leading chaplains in the New Model Army from 1645 to 1648.[9] Peters and Dell probably entered the Army during the summer of 1644,[10] but little was heard of their activities before Naseby. After that crushing defeat for the King's forces, both chaplains served at Langport, Bridgewater, Bristol, Winchester, Basing, Dartmouth, and Exeter, and in Cornwall.[11] Saltmarsh did not enter the Army until after January 1646.[12] Two other prominent chaplains, William Erbury[13] and William Sedgwick, had seen service for several years when the Presbyterians were still predominant in the Army. Edward Bowles, the last of the Presbyterian chaplains, left the Army shortly after Naseby, and his position at headquarters was taken by Dell. Saltmarsh and Peters also were attached directly to the headquarters staff of the Army and not to any particular regiment (as had been more common before 1645). However, a few chaplains were still attached directly to particular regiments: Baxter to Colonel Whalley's regiment, Erbury to Major-General Skippon's, Henry Pinnell to Colonel Pickering's, and Robert Ram to Colonel Rossiter's.

In addition to the official chaplains, there were numerous ministers who preached to the Army on various occasions. Possibly some had a claim to the title of chaplain, among them Joshua Sprigge, John Webster, Walter Cradock, and Richard Symonds;[14] others were Thomas Collier, Vavasor Powell, and the cornet Henry Denne.[15] Still another group were the numerous unordained ministers, the tradesmen or "mechanicks" as they were called, who preached when the Spirit moved them. The prevalence in the Army of these lay preachers is attested by Clarendon's observation that the common soldiers as well as the officers not only prayed and preached among themselves but went into the pulpits of churches and preached all kinds of religious opinions to the congregations.[16] Thomas Collier strongly espoused "mechanick" preaching by cobblers, tailors, tinkers, plowmen, and carpenters,[17] and a newssheet writer in 1650 printed the following verse:

> The graver Cobler shall expound
> and quote them Dell and Peters.[18]

In response to lay preaching the Presbyterian Parliament passed an ordinance on 26 April 1645 prohibiting sermons by anyone other than an ordained minister in "this or some other Reformed Church." Fairfax was ordered to enforce the ordinance in the Army strictly, but, as one pamphleteer put it, that does not mean that you cannot "both *pray* and *speak* . . . in such Orations, in such Liberties of speech, as may best enspirit the men that follow you . . . with such a religious and undaunted animation as may render them unconquerable before the proudest enemy."[19]

Significant among the efforts which contributed to the new religious spirit were the manifold services that the chaplains, both staff and regimental, rendered to the Army. One of the most important of these services, besides the regular sermons preached to the Army on the Sabbath, was the preaching on the eve of battle. On these occasions the chaplains exhorted the soldiers to persevere until final victory. For example, before the battle of Dartmouth on 19 January 1646, the weekly newssheet *The Moderate Intelligencer* (No. 47) observed that "Mr. *Peters,* and Mr. *Dell,* the most eminent Orators and Ecclesiasticks, whose influence uses to be authoratative upon the souldiers, made learned and affectionate Orations to them, assuring all such as shewed valour in that action . . . great reward." About seven o'clock in the evening the soldiers were drawn out into the field, the word was passed, "God with us," and the battle was on.[20] A broadsheet entitled *Don Pedro de Quixot* (1660) conceded that Saltmarsh not only possessed an excellent faculty for persuading the Army but also enjoyed a very great position of authority among the soldiers.

Once the Army was victorious in battle, and since the formation of the New Model this was the rule, the chaplains turned their attention from the Army to the conquered town. For instance, after the battle at Torrington in Devon in mid-February, 1646, Peters preached to a large audience from a balcony in the market place because the church had been blown up. Bulstrode Whitelock recorded in his *Memorials* that Peters on this occasion convinced many of their error in adhering to the King.[21] This was the Army's "Ubiquitary," who, together with the other chaplains, rode into Kent, Sussex, Berkshire, Buckinghamshire, Cornwall, and Wales "to stir them up to chuse good Parliament men."[22] In any captured town which sent members to Parliament, according to one pamphleteer, Peters, Dell, and Saltmarsh fell in with all the local faction and obtained one man "to promote their ambitious party."[23] It was Peters, writing of his own diplomatic assignment in his native Cornwall, who applied at Fairfax's behest all the expedients he could think of in order to stop eastern Cornwall from joining with the King's cavalry.[24] It was Peters again who still had energy to dash back to the Army to conduct, along with Dell, a fast day designed to seek God's blessing after the success of the Army's operations against the enemy at Bristol.[25]

The chaplains were frequently called upon to deliver concise reports in person to the House of Commons on the progress of the Army. These reports usually followed immediately after a major military engagement with the forces of the King. Both Fairfax and Cromwell employed the chaplains as news emissaries (what Sir Charles Firth called the equivalent of our modern war correspondents) to keep Parliament informed of the prisoners, ordnance, provisions, and towns taken in battle, to disclose the content of intercepted letters, and to present to the House gifts and trophies seized as prizes of war.[26] The House of Commons occasionally indicated its gratitude by rewarding its informants with substantial monetary grants.[27]

The most important duty that the chaplains performed,

however, was caring for the spiritual welfare of the troops, and their chief means to this end was their many sermons. The month prior to the surrender of the King's forces to Sir Thomas Fairfax at Oxford on 24 June 1646 may be taken as typical. On 25 May Saltmarsh preached before Fairfax and the soldiers at Headington; on the previous day, the Sabbath, Dell had preached in the forenoon and William Sedgwick[28] in the afternoon. According to the newsletter *Perfect Occurrences*, "many souldiers were at each sermon, divers of them climbing up into trees to hear (for it was in the Orchard before His Excellencies Tent) and it is very observable to consider the love and unity which is amongst the souldiers." The same newsletter reported that two Sundays later General Fairfax had established his headquarters at Mr. Crooke's house adjacent to St. Nicholas church in Marston overlooking the city of Oxford. Here on 7 June he negotiated with the commissioners from the beleaguered city. In the morning Fairfax listened to a sermon by Dell; in the afternoon he listened to a sermon by Saltmarsh.[29]

Among those present in the Marston church that Sunday morning were several citizens from London who were visiting for the first time what they thought would be the last Army encampment. Because there was to be no sermon at Wheatley, where they were staying, they decided to attend Dell's sermon, inasmuch as he was going to preach before General Fairfax. Following the sermon several of these citizens gathered around Dell to express their disapproval of his remarks. Dell later observed that "*suddenly they grew* fierce *and* furious contradicting and blaspheming, *yea,* some *of them* speaking *the language of* Hell *upon* Earth."[30] Thinking little more of the incident, Dell performed on 15 June the marriage ceremony between Henry Ireton, the Commissary-General, and Bridget Cromwell, the Lieutenant-General's eldest daughter.[31] Two weeks later, however, Dell was summoned before the House of Lords for allegedly having preached in his Marston sermon that "the power is in you the people; keep it part not with it." When Dell appeared before the Lords, the foregoing allegation, together with "heads" or other summaries of his Marston sermon, was read before the House.[32] Dell appealed for the dismissal of his case, but on 8 July the Lords ordered the committee that had been appointed to draw up charges against John Lilburne also to draw up charges against Dell. This was not the only time that Dell's name was associated with Lilburne's. Thomas Edwards was to call them both Anabaptist sectaries not unlike John of Leyden and Thomas Münzer, and William Prynne called Lilburne one of Dell's saints, arguing that they both advanced *"seditious anarchiall Positions."*[33] Three days later, on 11 July, the Lords ordered that Lilburne be imprisoned and fined, and that two of his tracts, *The Just Mans Justification* and *The Free-Mans Freedoms,* be burned. No such fate as this was in store for Dell, however, for on 17 July he was excused from daily attendance at the House, and he was never summoned to appear before it again.[34]

Through their preaching, in addition to the numerous other duties they performed, the Army preachers furthered the interests of the New Model. As the official religious spokesmen for the Army, the chaplains were able both to influence and to reflect the point of view of Cromwell and the headquarters staff, particularly in reference to religious matters. However, on political matters, as will be seen, some of them became extremely critical of the views of the "Grandees" or Army leaders toward the Levellers, and ultimately they left the Army for this reason. We shall next consider to what extent the chaplains were successful in imparting their religious views to the rest of the Army.

AN ARMY OF SAINTS

It is fairly easy to conjure up in the imagination a picture of the New Model Army as a Bible-reading, Psalm-singing soldiery which forsook shops and fields for pikes and muskets in support of the Parliamentary cause. Such intimations of piety are borne out to some extent in the writings of the chaplains of the New Model. Indeed, for Cromwell and the Army chaplains the Civil War was primarily a religious struggle. "Religion was not the thing at first contested for," said Cromwell, "but God brought it to that issue at last; and gave it unto us by redundancy; and at last it proved that which was most dear to us."[35] Not only were the issues religious ones, but from the point of view of the chaplains the soldiers were religious also. In a message delivered to both Houses of Parliament, Peters discussed what he felt was the most singular aspect of the New Model. In other armies most men forfeited their civility, observed Peters, whereas in the New Model men grew more religious than in any other place in the kingdom. As Saltmarsh put it, "God is amongst them." Dell also felt that there was more of the presence of God in the New Model than among any other group of people he had ever conversed with in his life, or, he was confident, any other gathering of men in all the world.

> *The Lord hath* poured forth [the Spirit of Prayer] *upon* many *of them in* great measure; *not only upon* many *of the* chief Commanders, *but on* very many *of the* inferior Officers, *and* common Troopers; some of *whom, I have by* accident *heard* praying, *with that* faith *and* familiarity *with God, that I have stood* wondring *at the* grace.[36]

It was not only the chaplains that felt this way. Two Royalists, William Chillingworth and Clarendon, found a great deal more piety and sobriety among the officers and soldiers of the Parliamentary Army than among the King's troops.[37]

Despite these views it is quite doubtful that the rank and file of the New Model Army were as deeply imbued with religious ideas as the chaplains contended. Two cogent arguments to this effect may be cited: the use of impressment in addition to voluntary enlistment, and the plundering of churches. The second argument is not unanswerable; the desecration of churches was actually defended by chaplain Robert Ram[38] as

being essentially an expression of intolerance toward Anglicanism—i.e., toward superstition and idolatry—growing out of an
ardent desire for more simplified ecclesiastical forms. The
impressment argument is much stronger. Five Parliamentary
ordinances from February to June, 1645, dealt with the impressment of men for the Parliamentary forces. On 12 May the
Venetian ambassador commented that the violence and force
used by Parliament to compel men to serve in the Army was
"cooling off" the favor of the common people.[39] Peters, while
making no claims for their religiosity, noted how serviceable
the worst of the impressed men had been under the example
of the other soldiers. General Fairfax observed that good soldiers had come out of the King's Army after the surrender of
the Royalist garrisons.[40] Good impressed soldiers, although
not by definition irreligious, could hardly have been inspired
by the same religious zeal, at least to begin with, which had
prompted others to volunteer.

It has been suggested that the "Godly Party" in the Army,
those whom Baxter identified as sectaries, brought the question
of pay to the foreground in the beginning as an issue that would
more readily unite the Army against the Presbyterian Parliament than religious or political issues, about which large numbers of soldiers cared little.[41] There is little doubt that financial
grievances were extremely important in the thinking of the
Parliamentary soldiers. However, with respect to pay in arrears, we know from Peters' report from Winchester castle that
pay had been behind as far back as October 1645, although it
is true that the question of a permanent settlement had not then
arisen.[42] Yet if this had been the sole issue, if the Parliamentary
soldiers included in effect only mercenaries and not saints of
the Lord, the Presbyterian Parliament could have paid off the
common soldiers, albeit with some difficulty.[43] The rank and
file thus would have melted away from the officers. The common soldiers, being less educated, were less verbal; they wrote
far fewer tracts than did the officers and chaplains; hence they

may have seemed less interested in religion or anything else.[44] Also, the kind of antiprofessional religion (anticlerical, antiprofessorial, and antilegal), which the chaplains advocated and which always allowed for "mechanick" preaching, found strength through its appeal to the uneducated rank and file. The chaplains had little respect for formal religious training in achieving salvation. For Dell it was every bit as easy for a poor "mechanick" to become persuaded of Christ's love through the Holy Spirit as it was for a nobleman or the King, or, he might have added, for an officer!

Just how many of the soldiery were imbued with religious ideas (or to what extent) is impossible to determine. It must not be forgotten that the few chaplains were largely occupied with their duties at the headquarters of the Army. Even with the assistance of occasional ministers and "mechanicks" it is difficult to see how they could have had the time and energy to preach a religion of the Spirit to thousands of men (many of them serving against their will) camped and garrisoned in many different places. It can be said that time and companionship in arms did bring a homogeneity of religious belief to those who were receptive to the ministrations of the Army's chaplains. This led the chaplains, at least, to look upon the soldiery as an army of saints. The differences with a predominantly Presbyterian Parliament over religious and political matters which were so important to the officers and chaplains, and the differences with Parliament over monetary matters which were so important to the rank and file, coincided to weld the Army into a solid front against the hostile Parliament.

PUTNEY PROJECTS

Once the Civil War was over, it seemed feasible to Parliament to reduce the size of the New Model and to dispatch a force of soldiers to reconquer Ireland. In March 1647, commissioners arrived at Saffron Walden to carry out Parliament's wishes. Immediately at the headquarters of the Army a new demand went up for payment of wages in arrears as well as an indemnity for acts performed in time of war. Although the pay of the infantry was eighteen weeks behind, and that of the horse and dragoons forty-three weeks, Parliament offered to pay only six weeks in cash upon discharge.[45] When the soldiers petitioned for payment for their services, freedom from future impressment for volunteers, and provision for the wounded, widows, and orphans, Parliament denounced the petitioners and threatened to proceed against them as enemies of the state. A little more than two months later Parliament made a further attempt at disbanding the Army. On 5 June the Army encamped near Newmarket and issued *A Solemn Engagement*. In this revolutionary paper the Army bound itself not to disband until its grievances had been redressed to the satisfaction of a council consisting of the general officers plus two commissioned officers and two soldiers to be chosen for each regiment. It was this council of agents or agitators which was to stage the debates at Putney four months later over the Leveller document, *An Agreement of the People*.

On 14 June there appeared a manifesto by Henry Ireton called *The Declaration of the Army*, which proclaimed that the New Model was no mere mercenary army to be hired out to serve any arbitrary power. Instead it was called forth to defend the people's rights and liberties. The Army, continued the *Declaration*, disowned any plan to overthrow Presbyterianism and urged any who differed from the established forms of church government not to be debarred from the rights and liberties belonging to all men equally under the commonwealth. The followers of John Lilburne in the Army, those known as the Levellers, must have heartily agreed with this statement of religious liberty, but they must have had some misgivings about another passage in the *Declaration* which stated that only those men should be given positions of power and trust who could be approved for moral righteousness and who acted by a principle of conscience and religion.[46]

The Declaration of the Army was followed two days later by the appearance of a list of eleven Presbyterians whom the Army demanded that the House of Commons expel. On 26 June the eleven members withdrew from the House. Exactly a month later a mob of reformadoes (disbanded soldiers) and apprentices, sympathetic to Presbyterianism, invaded the Houses of Parliament, forced them to rescind their conciliatory votes to the Army, and drove out about sixty members who fled to the New Model for safety. At this turn of events the eleven Presbyterian members returned. On 6 August the Army, accompanied by the sixty members, marched on London to begin a peaceful military occupation of the capital. Upon their arrival at the Houses of Parliament, Dell led them in prayers.[47] The Army's bloodless victory over Parliament still left a constitutional settlement to be made with the King, who had been seized by Cornet Joyce at Holmby on 4 June 1647. An attempt at settlement had been made on 1 August by the officers of the Army Council with the instrument known as *The Heads of Proposals.* In addition to biennial Parliaments, a Council of State, and social remedies against some excises, monopolies, tithes, and imprisonment for debt, the *Proposals* advocated relaxation of the coercive power of the magistrate toward the Book of Common Prayer and the Solemn League and Covenant, plus the payment of pay in arrears. But like most other constitutional proposals, the *Heads* proved unacceptable to Charles.

Early in October the dissatisfaction of the Levellers and some of the agitators with the Army's declarations and remonstrances of the preceding months was embodied in a tract by John Wildman entitled *The Case of the Army Truly Stated,* which was presented to General Fairfax by the agitators of five of the cavalry regiments.[48] This manifesto duplicated the statement of social grievances of *The Heads of Proposals* as well as many of its recommendations, but it made a radical departure from the *Heads* in its argument that Parliament was established by a paramount law and should be elected by manhood suffrage. Furthermore, it tacitly abrogated the power of the King and the House of Lords when it stated that all power was originally in the whole body of the people of the nation, and that the people's free choice as voiced by their representatives was the only foundation of just government.[49] In late October the Levellers drafted a platform of political beliefs, incorporating essentially the ideas of *The Case of the Army Truly Stated,* known as the first *Agreement of the People.* In the course of the debates over this platform held from 26 to 28 October at Putney church, essential differences between the ideas of the high officers (Cromwell and Ireton) and the Levellers (Wildman, Rainborough, and others) became apparent. This cleavage also divided chaplains Saltmarsh and Peters.

The basic issue in dispute between Ireton and Rainborough arose out of Article I of the *Agreement of the People.* The question was whether or not only those with "a permanent fixed interest in the kingdom" should be allowed to vote, i.e., whether or not only the forty-shilling freeholders should constitute the body politic. If a wider franchise were granted, some felt, all property would be destroyed. But the great mass of Englishmen, who were merely tenants at will, found their spokesman in Colonel Rainborough, who argued: "the poorest he that is in England hath a life to live, as the greatest he." "If we had not a right to the kingdom," added the agitator Edward Sexby, "we were mere mercenary soldiers."[50] As the debate between customary rights and natural rights proceeded, both Saltmarsh and Peters among the chaplains expressed their opinions.

Saltmarsh, who was absent from the Debates, sent his views to the Council of War in a letter which Captain Bishop said ought to be read to the assemblage. In the letter Saltmarsh admonished the Council for not having discharged itself to the people "in such things as they justly expected from ye." He undoubtedly had in mind the *Solemn Engagement* of the Army

of 5 June 1647, in which the soldiers and officers bound themselves together not to disband until their grievances had been
redressed. In a letter to Fairfax on 30 October he wrote:

> Stop not the breathings of God in meane private Christians;
> the counsells of God flow there, when the greater persons
> sometimes (for his glory) are left naked without a word of
> advice from him. I found this desolate evill beginning in
> your meetings. Be faithfull to your ingagement for Justice
> to the Kingdome: you have many, and you promised many
> things . . . where you have been unrighteous, delatory, or
> unfaithfull . . . depart out of those tents, least God over-
> take you.

Peters made a rather unusual proposal which did not receive
any consideration for solving the suffrage issue: "I hope it is
not denied by any man that any wise, discreet man that hath
preserved England [is worthy of a voice] in the government of
it." What standards would be imposed to screen the "wise" and
"discreet," Peters never set forth; it is apparent, however, that
he would limit the franchise to a fraction of those soldier-saints
who had fought in the Parliamentary Army.[51] On 8 November
the agitators were sent back to their regiments, but a week later
mutiny had broken out in the ranks of the New Model Army.

At Corkbush Field near Ware, an encampment for about
one-third of the Army, a manifesto was issued on 14 November
requiring a pledge of loyalty to Fairfax and the Army Council.
The regiments of Robert Lilburne and Thomas Harrison did
not take the pledge. On the following day they appeared on
the field with the copies of the *Agreement of the People* stuck
in their hats. Realizing that military discipline had nearly col-
lapsed, Cromwell ordered that the copies be removed. The
soldiers obeyed his order. The ringleaders of the mutiny were
promptly condemned by a court-martial; one was shot, and
others, including Colonel Ayres, Major Cobbet, and Captain
Bray, were imprisoned.[52] A few days later the Army moved its
headquarters to Windsor.

In early December Saltmarsh left his home in Yelford, Essex, and appeared at the encampment of the Army at Windsor "as one risen from the grave." Thomas Fuller, whose sermon at the Church of the Savoy on 26 July 1643 Saltmarsh had attacked in his *Examinations,* claimed that the Army chaplain was suffering from a "disease, which had seized his intellectuals." Saltmarsh told the General Council of Officers that although the Lord had done much for them in the past, He had now forsaken their councils because they had imprisoned the faithful ones, the Levellers, at Corkbush Field. Saltmarsh praised the tenderness in Peters' spirit but added that Peters had been misled by others and had wrongly allowed his heart to be hardened by them. To Cromwell, his former commander, Saltmarsh proclaimed that the Lord was very angry with him for causing godly men to be imprisoned, slighted, and abused for beliefs which he himself had formerly held. Without doffing his hat, he further told Cromwell to release the imprisoned members of the Army and refrain from prosecuting those men who had been so faithful. Cromwell's only reply was a statement that he had received a letter from a "Mr. S." which said about the same thing.[53] After Saltmarsh had delivered his message he took his last leave of the Army and returned home. His departure was the beginning of an exodus of chaplains from the New Model. At home he told his wife that he had now finished his work and must go to his Father. He died the following day.[54]

The "Mr. S." to whom Cromwell referred may have been another chaplain, William Sedgwick. According to John Lilburne, Sedgwick had joined "precious Mr. Saltmarsh" in denouncing the actions of the "New Tyrants the Grandees" of the Army for imprisoning the soldiers at Windsor.[55] Sedgwick wrote a letter to Fairfax condemning the General for obstinately refusing the Word of the Lord: "You must remember my sermon to you at Windsor upon that Text. Overturn, overturn, overturn; 'tis Scripture still, and that word lives in and upon you. *Saltmarsh* his message quickly followed it, *Depart from the tents* of these *unrighteous men,* he lives still."[56]   In the *Clarke Papers* there is a letter from a London correspondent to a friend in the Army on 30 March 1647 announcing that Sedgwick had arrived in the capital and prophesied that the world was coming to an end within fourteen days.[57]   Toward the end of 1647 "Doomsday Sedgwick," as he was now called, went to Carisbrooke castle on the Isle of Wight to interview the captive Charles I.   According to Wood, Sedgwick presented His Majesty with a copy of his book, *The Leaves of the Tree of Life.* The King, after having read a small portion of it, observed: *"the Author stands in some need of sleep."*[58]   The book upbraided the Army for not doing good for all instead of advancing a party and a faction.   "So your cause is lost," wrote Sedgwick, "and you only fight because you are an Army; *because fighting is your business."*   And again: "Now you are the *last, and heaviest* of the *Nations* burthens; that promised to save and deliver, *and turne the greatest Tyrants; lose all the good you have done; set up a forcible Government; turne warre into a trade, England into a Campe, perpetuate desteruction, and provoak new commotions."*[59]

If these diatribes of Saltmarsh and Sedgwick confounded and amazed the Army leaders, as Lilburne recorded,[60] they also stimulated the distracted Henry Pinnell, chaplain in the regiment of Colonel Pickering.   Pinnell later wrote how he was tempted by Satan to put forward base motives of pride and vainglory in order to get a name, be noticed, win popular applause, and become famous like Saltmarsh and Sedgwick.   And as he walked in his self-admitted wilderness of confusion and distraction he heard "the Voice cryed by Mr. *Sedgwick* and Mr. *Saltmarsh,* Forsake, Forsake, and come out of these crooked and carnall way.es and pathes, and come into more strict and spirituall courses and enjoyments."   On 11 December Pinnell left London for Windsor in order to convey his thoughts to Cromwell.   He praised the Lieutenant-General for refusing to disband the Army and for enjoining the Army to do justice and

relieve the oppressed, but he added that Cromwell had neglected to do what he promised, so that now the kingdom cried
and groaned under neglect just as much as under former
oppressions.[61]

The exodus of some of the chaplains of the New Model Army
prompted a barbed intelligencer for the newssheet *Mercurius
Melancholicus,* in mid-January 1648, to inquire: "I wonder
what's become of [the Army's] horse-Preachers in red caps, and
plush jackets, what are they silenced? or hath shame and good
manners better taught the snivelling Johnneyes?" By March,
Dell, too, had severed his connection with the New Model
Army. During the next month Major John Jubbes became convinced that the Army was laying the foundations of a "lasting"
war. "I thereat laid down my sword," Jubbes wrote later, "and
at the sad thing then appearing, pretious Mr. *Saltmarsh* his
life, Mr. *Penell,* Mr. *Dell* and others left the Army."[62]

As early as January 1648 the Council of the Army, having
gained information that several godly ministers wished to
preach the gospel in the Army, decided to make some additions
to the depleted number of Army chaplains. Whether the Council's action was taken in order to revert to the previous system
of a chaplain for each regiment, as Firth suggested, or whether
it was to recruit replacements for the departing chaplains, is
not clear. Some indication of a "changing of the guard" among
the chaplains was given about a week later in the pro-Royalist
newssheet *Mercurius Elencticus,* which reported that Cromwell
had sent for twelve more ministers in order to preserve the
Army from further schism.[63]

The brief but crucial span of dominance in Army circles of
the Antinomian preachers had come to an end. What did they
have besides their Army experiences in common? When they
finally broke with the "Grandees," their sympathies were
clearly with the activities of the Levellers, except for Hugh
Peters, who remained loyal to the "Grandees." Admittedly, the

evidence regarding the chaplains in these important events is scanty and not always too clear. We shall accordingly examine in the next chapter whether or not there was anything in their theological views which may have inclined them to side with the Levellers. We shall also examine the theological views of Peters and Baxter, both of whom were staunch opponents of Leveller ideas.

Most of the Army preachers believed that the New Model was an army of saints who were possessed by the Holy Spirit and were thus assured of their own salvation—to the point of believing that they were victorious in battle because God had been in the midst of them.[64] "If God be for us," ran the text from Romans 8:31, "who can be against us?"

However, to certain enemies of the Army such as Robert Baillie, Thomas Edwards, Christopher Love, William Prynne, and Samuel Rutherford, it seemed obvious that if God gave men the strength and power to triumph over the forces of the King, there was surely nothing to prevent God (through his vessels filled with the Holy Spirit) from destroying the Army's other antagonists—the Presbyterian Parliament, for example. For that matter, there was nothing to prevent God from turning to other subjects such as the question of the political privileges of the saints. It is only natural that these enemies of the preachers should assail them for disseminating "seditious" ideas. "When wee daily heare and read what *Peters, Saltmarsh, Dell* &c. those worthy Saints both preach and print, *and what gallant Fellowes they have now with the sword in their hands, and what priviledges they clayme unto themselves,* it is a matter of wonder and astonishment to me, that they are not all of them timely looked unto."[65] In the following pages a belated attempt will be made to comply with this request.

Antinomianism Anatomized

English Puritans in the sixteenth century held that the Bible was a complete body of laws and conduct—the sole source of authority between man and God. They also affirmed the absolute and complete sovereignty of God, whose will, as revealed in the Bible, was law to be absolutely obeyed. In Geneva during the reign of Queen Mary some of them were plied with the old wine of Pauline-Augustinian piety in new Calvinist bottles. From the eighth chapter of the Book of Romans they read the central dogma of Pauline theology: God in his inscrutable wisdom, through his free grace and mercy, had predestined some people to eternal salvation and the rest to eternal damnation. In his *Institutes* John Calvin defended the justice of God's immutable decrees; however, he refused to make the Augustinian distinction between foreknowing and foreordaining—between prescience and necessity.[1] By failing to do this, he exposed himself to the following criticism, succinctly stated later by John Milton: obedience to something that cannot be disobeyed is an empty pursuit.[2] Carried to the extreme by such Genevan exiles as Christopher Goodman and John Knox, resistance to tyrants was justified in the name of obedience to God. However, the doctrine of revolt rapidly became, as did Queen Mary who had in part provoked it, an anomaly of late Tudor and early Stuart England.

Goodman and Knox wrote from Calvin's Geneva, but John Ponet, who also had stressed the right of resistance, was no Calvinist and wrote from Strassburg. It was in Strassburg and Zwingli's Zurich that others of the Marian exiles were attracted to a Covenant theology, which was not fundamental to Calvin's view.[3] Covenant theology had already made important strides in the reign of Edward VI, when a number of famous Rhineland leaders, including Peter Martyr and Martin Bucer, visited England; it appears to have crystallized in England by 1580 and to have become normative for English Puritanism during the early decades of the seventeenth century. The difference with Calvin was this: whereas Calvin thought of the covenant of grace as already completely fulfilled by God, the Rhineland reformers thought of the covenant as a contract of mutual obligation entered into voluntarily by God and man for man's salvation. Although God assumed the initiative by providing the grace that made possible man's power of belief, God demanded in return only a pledge that, when grace was given to man, he would make use of this grace which made faith possible. The Federal Covenant theologians did not advocate free will as such, but they did state that man had only himself to blame if he refused the initiative taken by God. This Federal theology had its counterparts in church and political covenants, the latter providing a theological base for the social contract.[4]

The Federal theologians steadfastly resisted the temptation to justify the ways of God to man by a reliance upon free will, guided by right reason, in accepting or rejecting God's grace. This point of view received its classic formulation in the Five Articles of the Remonstrance addressed in 1610 to the States-General of Holland and West Friesland. The Remonstrants, disciples of Arminius, made salvation contingent upon the good works of man, whereas in the Federal theory good works are not a cause but an accompaniment of salvation.[5] At the Synod of Dort in 1618–19 the ideas of the Arminians were condemned; nevertheless, Dort had its effect upon Anglican clergymen. It was there that John Hales of Eaton bade "good-night to John Calvin." Within the next few years several Anglican bishops, notably Richard Neile and William Laud, were stigmatized by the Puritans as expositors of "Popery and Arminianism." In the pulpit, in the press, and in Parliament the Puritans attempted to identify these Arminians, at least in the public eye, with the small minority of Catholics. The theological views of the Laudian bishops, coupled with their attitude of ecclesiastical "decency" and a political view that sanctioned Charles I's "personal" rule, rendered the Anglican church vulnerable to the "root and branch" policies of the Long Parliament. Although Arminian views were not restricted to the Anglican hierarchy they remained odious to most Puritans.

Federal Covenant theology precariously hovered between Arminianism at one extreme and Antinomianism at the other. The Antinomians placed no trust in a covenant, good works, or the reason of man in achieving salvation. They relied solely on the Spirit or Free Grace of God. To them "the Free-Grace of Christ . . . *justifies a sinner before he believes, before any qualification in the world be wrought in him, and then afterward open his eyes, and gives him Faith and other qualifications."* In ascribing all to Free Grace (God's order, harmony, and perfection) and nothing to free will (human freedom)—all to piety and nothing to reason—the Antinomians asked why they should study the Commandments or fear condemnation for sins which had been completely taken away by Christ. In the words of one of the English progenitors of the doctrine of Free Grace, John Eaton, Christ's "righteousnesse wherewith he cloathes us, doth as perfectly abolish from before God all our sinnes, as the Sunbeames abolish darknesse out of a dark house."[7] Eaton was influenced by the work of John Everard, who had translated into English in 1628 the famous *Theologia Germanica*, a mystical religious work published by Luther. Eaton's views, supported by those of Giles Randall, grew stronger as the English nation took up arms to resolve the quarrels between King and Parliament.

The disintegration of Puritanism into sects and divisions was due partly to the collapse of episcopal authority, partly to the opposition that arose to Scottish Presbyterianism in both the

Long Parliament and the Westminster Assembly, and partly
to divisive tendencies within the movement itself, which did
not gain momentum, except for isolated groups such as the
Familists, until the 1640's. In 1643 Robert Baillie, a Scottish
Presbyterian sitting in the Assembly, observed that "the Independent partie grows but the Anabaptists more; and the Antinomians most." Within the New Model Army Baxter observed
that Antinomianism was the "predominant Infection."[8]

The term Antinomianism is slightly misleading when it is
applied to the religious views of the Army chaplains. It was
employed largely by their critics in order to connote the historical association of the term with licentiousness and anarchy.
As Dell put it, the "true" Antinomians were the libertines who
wanted to live just as they desired and who took their "full
swinge" in lust. However, when Saltmarsh was charged with
being an Antinomian, he replied: "If to say we serve not the
oldnesse of the Letter, but in the *newnesse* of the Spirit: If to
say . . . We are not under the Law, but under *Grace* . . . If
this be *Antinomianism*, I am one of that sort of Antinomians."[9]
Proponents of Free Grace have been called "spirit mystics" because of their belief in the indwelling spirit of God in man.[10]
They have been called "Finders" because they found what the
Seekers were looking for—the primitive Christian religion.[11]
They have even on occasion been referred to as "Free Gratians." Free Grace, wrote Baxter, was a "sugared" title for Antinomianism.[12]

Hugh Peters was very much concerned with the concept of
Free Grace, even though in New England he had been an adherent of the Federal Covenant theology and a harsh critic of
Antinomianism as expressed by Anne Hutchinson. According
to Haller, it was adherence to the doctrine of Free Grace that
released Peters from the confusion of doctrinal disputation and
freed him for revolutionary action.[13] The text of Peters' Thanks-
giving sermon before Parliament on 2 April 1646 was from

Psalms 31:23: "O love the Lord, all ye his saints: for the Lord preserveth the faithful, and plentifully rewardeth the proud doer." In a little book called *A Dying Fathers Last Legacy to an Only Child*, written just before his execution as a regicide in 1660, Peters mentioned that he had formerly delighted in speaking to others about Free Grace, and that he thought it was "the sum of true practical Divinity."[14] However, the full development of the doctrine of Free Grace came not from Peters but from the exegeses of Dell and Saltmarsh.

Although none of Saltmarsh's sermons are extant, he wrote and published prolifically during the last three years of his life, and from this corpus of writing may be found the substance of his ideas and convictions as he preached them to the Army at St. Mary's, Oxford, and elsewhere. Saltmarsh might well have chosen, on one of these occasions, the following scriptural texts from Romans 5:18–19:

18. Therefore as by the offence of one judgement came upon all men to condemnation; even so by the righteousness of one the free gift came upon all men unto justification of life.

19. For as by one man's disobedience many were made sinners, so by the obedience of one shall many be made righteous.

Certain words in these verses suggest the two main lines of analysis that will be followed in the balance of this chapter. The "free gift," which brought salvation to man through the righteousness of Christ, which absolved him from the original, imputed sin of Adam in the garden of Eden, and which freed him from the bondage of the covenant of works formulated in the tablets of stone by Moses, was the same thing that Peters and Saltmarsh termed Free Grace. The words "all men" in the eighteenth verse suggest a universal principle of salvation which, to be sure, is considerably mitigated by the reference only to "many" men set forth in the nineteenth verse. But "universal grace," as we shall see, was one of the heresies that Baxter found in the writings of Saltmarsh.

In his book entitled *Free-Grace*, written in 1646, Saltmarsh wrote that free justification by grace meant:

> A BELEEVER in all of his dealings with God either by Prayer, or other way of drawing neer, is to state, and consider himself thus in *Christ* in the first place, and to put on the relation of *Sonship* and Righteousnesse, and to look at or consider sin no otherwise in himself then as debts paid and cancelled by the blood of Christ; and by this all *bondages, fears,* and *doubtings* are removed, and his *Spirit* is free; *For the son hath made him free*: And now he comes in the spirit of adoption, and calls God *Father*; and here begins all *faith, hope, confidence, love, liberty.*

In other words, the saving grace of God, which sets the believer spiritually free through Christ, is given to him as a sinner, and no condition of repentance, or humbleness, or obedience is required for that justification before God. For if any of these conditions were required, then it would be a Popish doctrine of justification by works. In fact, Saltmarsh asserted that regeneration through Christ had come to believers without any acts of faith, obedience, and repentance on their part.[15]

It becomes readily apparent upon the slightest examination of Dell's published sermons that he also placed extreme emphasis in his theology upon the third person of the Holy Trinity. The power of the Holy Spirit or grace, unassisted by any works on the part of man, transformed the elect or saints of God from sinning, carnal children of Adam into justified brothers and sisters in Christ. "Thus the power of the Spirit changes our whole corrupt nature, and makes it conformable to the Divine nature; as Fire makes the Iron in which it prevails, like unto itself, communicating its own nature to it." Just as the iron contributes nothing to the heat of the fire, so the elect of God contribute nothing to the reception and entertainment of the Spirit within their own souls. The sweeping of sin from the soul by the Spirit is then followed by the strewing of the soul with grace. This process of emptying and filling, in which the children of light have the nearest union with the Son of God that any mortal can have, is accomplished by prayer, hearing the word of God preached, and faith.[16]

The Antinomians believed that faith was not a *condition* of salvation to be fulfilled by man. According to Collier, "God gives faith to beleeve, for *faith is the* gift of God."[17] Whether or not one had the power to believe was entirely dependent upon whether or not one had been given faith by the Holy Spirit. As Saltmarsh wrote: "Faith is truely and simply this: *A being* perswaded more or lesse of Christs love; and therefore it is called, *A Beleeving with the heart* . . . . *but none can simply perswade a soul that it doth beleeve, but he on whom it doth beleeve*."[18] Such statements of God's grace and man's faith implied a doctrine of divine determinism which would endanger every phase of human responsibility in cleansing man from sin and justifying him through the Spirit before God. Saltmarsh, Dell, and Collier exhorted the faithful to leave off from the operations of their own minds, understandings, wills, and affections. They preached in effect a denial of self, a denial of the sufficiency of man's creatureliness. From Luke 22:42 came the text "not my will but thine be done." All the work of salvation must be attributed to Christ. "It is not I that live," wrote Dell, "but Christ *himself* that lives in me." In such a fashion man is brought closer to God and arrives at the highest mystery—"the deniall of our selves."[19]

This mystical element among the Antinomian chaplains was an expression of Puritan pietism, which can be divided, according to Winthrop Hudson, into two strains. The one was not hostile to the use of reason in religion; it worked within the conventional church groupings, and it finally culminated in the

Cambridge Platonists of the Restoration. The other strain, which best accommodates Dell, Saltmarsh, and Collier, attributed all things to the Holy Spirit and denied the importance of outward forms and ceremonies of the church, a position very like that of George Fox and the Quakers.[20]

Oliver Cromwell, according to Haller, was the greatest witness to the doctrine of Free Grace as preached by Dell, Saltmarsh, and Peters. After the New Model's victory at Naseby, Cromwell, never one to debate fine points of theological doctrine, wrote to William Lenthall, the Speaker of the House of Commons: "Sir, this is none other but the Hand of God; and to Him alone belongs the glory, wherein none are to share with Him." And a month later, after the victory at Langport, Cromwell wrote to a member of the House of Commons: "Thus you see what the Lord hath wrought for us. Can any creature ascribe anything to itself? Now can we give the glory to God, and desire all may do so, for it is all due unto Him!"[21]

It is one thing, however, to attribute everything to God and nothing to man, and quite another thing to be able to distinguish between the spirit of God and "carnal reasoning" in man. Dell realized that everyone must have the skill to differentiate between those gifts that are natural to himself and those that flow from God's Spirit. If you can detect natural abilities, wisdom, or academic learning in yourself, he said, then you can be sure of nothing but deformity, darkness, and death, but in the gifts that flow from God's Spirit, you can see only heavenly beauty, luster, and glory.[22] With the question stated in this way (i.e., where does God leave off and man begin?) Dell's concept of faith became, in the eyes of its critics, a very subjective affair—the work of the human conscience unhampered by ecclesiastical authority or the letter of the Scriptures. Even Cromwell, sympathetic as he was to many of the views of the Army chaplains, foresaw this problem. Speaking at the Army Debates at Putney late in 1647 he said: "I know a man may answer all difficulties, really where itt is, but wee are very apt all of us to call that faith, that perhaps may bee butt carnall imagination, and carnall reasonings."²³ And, as all those present at the Putney Debates could testify, the imaginations and reasonings of men could indeed vary a great deal.

A further extension of the doctrine of the indwelling Spirit, in which the will and reason of man were negated, was a belief in the perfectibility—though not the perfection—of man. "As long as the Spirit of God dwells in the Flesh," wrote Dell, "it will still be reforming the Flesh to the Spirit, till the whole body of Sin be destroyed . . . till all be perfected."²⁴ Yet the Antinomi. ns did not go so far as to say that this perfection had been, or was about to be, achieved. Henry Denne and Thomas Collier, for example, qualified their views on perfectionism by saying that man still sins in the flesh, but not in the conscience. Hence, we do not *willingly* sin. Saltmarsh made a different kind of distinction. He said that whereas a believer's sins can never separate him from God, they can separate him from communion with God.²⁵ But the critics of the Antinomians saw nothing but casuistry in such qualifications. Rutherford wrote: "They say the Saints are perfect, and their works perfect. I slander them not, read Master *Towne*, M. *Eaton*, and *Saltmarsh*."²⁶

This tenet regarding the perfectibility of man, together with the heavy reliance upon the Holy Spirit to the exclusion of any covenant or pact between God and man, most strikingly differentiated the Antinomian chaplains from the Federal Covenant chaplains, Baxter and, to a lesser extent, Peters. Both sides agreed that Free Grace alone led to salvation, and that faith was the gift of God; both condemned the Arminian heresy of placing at least part of the means of salvation, usually good works, within the power of man. But the Federalists were reluctant to take man out of the scheme of salvation completely; therefore they framed their theology in terms of a covenant of mutual obligations. Peters wrote that the Free Grace he had spoken of should be considered mainly as the fruit of the "New Covenant," which rested upon two parties, Christ and the believer. The duties binding upon man in the covenant largely consisted of an acceptance of the grace of God. As Peters phrased it, union with Christ can never be achieved "till your *Understand-ing be enlightened* with the want of Christ, and His worth, and then that your Will be so subdued to that Light, that it draw forth choice, and consent of, and to that only good." Of course, if faith was not given by God, then man could not accept it. In that contingency, Peters saw the need to "hear, beg, pray, weep, fast, seek, labour, strive, use violence, read, ask, wish, sigh," in order to acquire faith. The Antinomians asked less of their followers.[27]

A concrete example may help to clarify the issue. Baxter liked to compare the covenant between man and God with the marriage contract between husband and wife. It is just as if you married a poor woman who has no worldly possessions, he said: you offer her yourself and all your possessions on the sole condition that she will consent to marry you. This is the ac-ceptance, the consent, the covenanting, and—Baxter added, perhaps facetiously—the self-resigning, for these are "in a man-ner all of one thing." But although mere consent is the only condition of first possession, yet the faithful performance of marriage duties by the wife—"not going in to others"—is neces-sary to continue the marriage.[28] The counterpart to Baxter's analogy in Saltmarsh's theology would be the case of an ab-ducted maiden. The maiden's fear would have been converted by her abductor's love to faith, and her startled incredulity at her own abduction would have changed to an assuring belief that it had really happened and was not just a wishful dream. The Baxter analogy was essentially legalistic; with Saltmarsh, it was outside the pale of the law.

It should be noted in the Saltmarsh analogy that "faith is a consequent of our justification," as Henry Denne put it, "and not an intercedent of justification."[29] Both Saltmarsh and Dell, despite their constant reiteration of faith as a belief worked in man by Free Grace alone, frequently spoke of believing—as dis-tinguished from faith—as if it were an act of the will or at least something that men could reject. "So as Christ is ours *without* faith . . . we cannot here *know* him to be ours by *beleeving*," wrote Saltmarsh, "nor partake of him as ours but by beleeving." Human responsibility begins here to qualify divine determinism. The rather fine theological point that Saltmarsh contended for was that the actual work of salvation had been done for believers when Christ was crucified on the cross, and that to be truly saved they need only believe that such a work had indeed been done in their behalf.[30]

> *Salvation* is not made any puzzeling work in the *Gospel;* it is *plainly, easily,* and *simply* revealed; *Jesus Christ was crucified* for *sinners;* this is *salvation,* we need go no further; the *work* of *salvation* is past, and finished; *sins* are *blotted out; sinners* are *justified* by him that *rose for justification.* And now if you ask me what you must *do to be saved,* I answer *Beleeve in the Lord Jesus Christ, and thou shalt be saved.* All that is to be done in the work of *salvation* is to *beleeve* there is such a *work,* and that *Christ died* for *thee,* amongst all those other *sinners* he *died* for.[31]

Critics were quick to point out what appeared to be casuistic distinctions in Antinomianism. In a vigorous polemic Thomas Gataker, a member of the Westminster Assembly, accused Saltmarsh of propounding the same *"conditions* of *receiving and taking* & *believing* on" for salvation that Saltmarsh himself had attacked in the "Legalists" or Federal Covenanters. And Gataker pressed what he felt was a logical inconsistency in Saltmarsh:

> *Christ* you say, *is ours without Faith; but we can not know him to be ours but by believing:* and you reject this under the Title of the *Reformed opinion and more generall, That none are justified or partakers of salvation, but by faith.* And if *no conditions* at all be required for obtaining *salvation* by Christ as was formerly affirmed by you, then neither *Faith* also.[32]

John Crandon also felt that Antinomian theology was contradictory. If justification is a free act of God without any condition on the part of man, how can it also be true that "bare beliefe in the narrowest sense" is also a necessary condition of man's justification? The answer lies in the distinction Saltmarsh made between a faith of adherence, which is what Christ worked in man, and a faith of assurance, which is the believing on the work of salvation done by Christ on the cross. This latter kind of faith followed after salvation and did not precede salvation. It was, as John Wallis phrased it, "a beleeving of a Proposition affirmed," rather than "an accepting of Christ offered" as the Federalists believed.[33]

The tenuous argument of Saltmarsh's version of Free Grace was viewed by Thomas Gataker as implying that faith was caused by justification, a reversal of the traditional Protestant doctrine of justification by faith. The view imputed to Saltmarsh was also held by Denne, who had written that men were justified by God *"before the act of our beleeving."*[34] Furthermore, Gataker could not concur with Saltmarsh that believers could be saved without first repenting of sin, since under these circumstances men could go on sinning with impunity.[35] Under these circumstances it would also be possible for untutored believers who might be genuinely convinced of their conversion to Christ to ignore the spirit as well as the letter of the law, divine or civil, and to follow the compulsions of their own wishes. Not so, replied the Antinomians: no man can take liberty to sin under a pretense of grace. Free Grace did not authorize licentiousness.[36]

In his confession of faith, published in 1655, Baxter admitted that he had ten years earlier been half-ensnared by the opinions about "Justification before Faith." He was ultimately disabused by his reading of Saltmarsh's *Free-Grace*, which he describes as "exceedingly taking" both within and without the Army. After a serious perusal and examination of the book, Baxter concluded that it was full of palpable errors. He accordingly judged it his duty to lend his support in the word-battle against the Antinomians, especially when he saw "how greedily multitudes of poor souls did take the bait."[37]

When Saltmarsh wrote that "we *beleeve, repent, love,* and obey . . . not that we may be saved, but because we are saved," he was stating the sharpest difference between the Antinomian and Covenant theologies. The Federalists believed that salvation was possible; the Antinomians believed that it had already come. In Baxter's view the true believer performed his duties *for* life and salvation and not *from* life and salvation. And to Baxter it did not make very much difference whether it was called the Spirit, or evidences, or faith, which produced salvation. That would be like asking whether it was the meat, or our stomach, or our teeth, or our hands that feed us: or whether it was by our eyesight or the sunlight that we see. They were distinct causes all necessary to produce the same effect.[38] For the Antinomians, by contrast, there was no question of cause and effect, no worry whether or not the conditions of the covenant had been fulfilled, no demonstrations of salvation to be made by a rational persuasion or argumentation, and no fretting over whether the sin of Adam in the garden of Eden had been completely removed. "I am already justified," wrote Collier, "and so made a son . . . of God." "We *work*, and *walk*, and *live* under the Gospel," wrote Saltmarsh, "as being *saved* already, and redeemed."[39]

Indeed, there was an overtone of this assurance of salvation in a letter from Oliver Cromwell on 25 October 1646 to his daughter Bridget. The Seekers, to whom the letter refers, rejected the apostolic succession and a national church, and were looking for the apostles who would usher in a new ecclesiastical era to be built by a new apostolic dispensation. (Most of the chaplains did not share this view: they felt that the truth was not to be found in any outward church ordinances, but had been found in the inward spiritualization of the visible church on earth by the Holy Spirit.) Cromwell wrote:

> Your Sister Claypole . . . sees her own vanity and carnal mind, bewailing it; she seeks after (as I hope also) that which will satisfy. And thus to be a seeker is to be of the best sect next to a finder; and such an one shall every faithful humble seeker be at the end. Happy seeker, happy finder![40]

Baxter was particularly disturbed by some of the implications of the "monstrous piece" of Antinomian doctrine which he found so prevalent in Saltmarsh and in the Army. If you believe, he argued, that righteousness is "in Christ, and not in our selves, or performed by Christ, and not by our selves," then you are blaspheming Christ—as if he had sin from which to repent or pardon to accept. And if Christ has fulfilled the new covenant of grace as well as the old covenant of the law, then any kind of believing, even a mere believing in a work already done, is meaningless, for what is the point of doing the same thing twice? Shall we come after God, wrote Baxter, to do the work He has perfected? Then he landed his hardest blow against the "unsavory stuff" in the book of *Free-Grace*. Saltmarsh implied, according to Baxter, that Jews and pagans and every man shall be saved. "Do not say that I odiously wring out these consequences," he continued; "they are as plain as can be expected."[41]

UNIVERSAL SALVATION

Most of the chaplains believed that Free Grace was actually granted by God only to those elect souls whom he had chosen and predestined before time began.[42] Thus, when the chaplains wrote of "believers," they were actually referring to the elect of God. This acceptance of an election of grace—this reduction of "all men" (Romans 5:18) to "many" men (5:19)[43]—indicates the doctrinal affinity on this point between the Antinomian concept of Free Grace and Calvinistic orthodoxy. If only some are saved, and not all, Saltmarsh inquired, why is it so contended that all men are redeemed?[44]

Saltmarsh provided a partial answer to his own query. He recognized that the use of such terms as "all" and "every man" as synonyms for believers or the elect "makes some stumble at the Election of some, and so conclude, *Redemption* for *all*."[45] Such a misuse of these words, though apparently quite unintentional, is indeed characteristic of Saltmarsh's own writing.

To those who could not believe that they were already saved because they had doubts that they were among the elect, he replied that no man could say he was not of the elect, since God's wisdom was inscrutable and his ways past finding out. Moreover, Saltmarsh argued, doubters were bound to believe that they were saved because God had so commanded. Knowledge that the keys to salvation are limited only to the elect should not prohibit *any* man from believing that he was saved.[46]

Rutherford concluded from a reading of *Free-Grace* that Saltmarsh not only held the opinion that Christ died for all the sins of all men, but also believed that all men were chosen to salvation. "There is here strong power in opinions," added Rutherford. Though Rutherford's inference is understandable, Saltmarsh had actually stated the problem a little differently: Christ had died only for the elect, but Christ's suffering was offered as an expiation of sin to all men so that the elect, who were among all men, might believe. "Though he died not for *all,* yet none are *excepted,* and yet none *accepted* but they that *beleeve,* and none beleeve but they to *whom it is given.*" Certainly Rutherford would have agreed with Saltmarsh that in this way of salvation there lies great mystery, although Rutherford would hardly have called it that. Saltmarsh defended his use of the word "excepted" here as the grounds for preaching the gospel to all men; i.e., offering Christ to all men.[47]

The same inference that Rutherford drew from *Free-Grace* was drawn by Thomas Gataker from different premises in the theology of Thomas Collier. Although Collier did not believe in universal salvation, he did maintain that Christ had died for all the sins of all men.[48] This assertion, said Gataker, did nothing but teach men to believe a lie, to wit, that God would save such men as indeed would never be saved. Furthermore, it encouraged the unreflecting "to run on hoodwinked, untill sodainly they fall headlong into hell."[49]

Erbury and Denne were also, and more justly, accused of believing in universal salvation. Erbury was charged by

Thomas Edwards with corrupting the soldiers of the Army with this doctrine, and he did indeed incline to such a view in his *Testimony,* a collection of writings published in 1658.[50] Denne had adhered to the doctrine of election in his earlier tract, *A Conference Between a Sick Man and a Minister* (1642), but in 1646 he boldly stated that the Lord had drawn everyone to himself at some time or other. If anyone remained a stranger to God, continued Denne, it was because he had eluded God's dragnet through his resistance to the Holy Spirit. Rutherford accused Denne of being both an Arminian and an Antinomian: an Arminian because he defended universal atonement and an Antinomian because he believed Christ loosened men from the law. Thomas Bedford felt that Denne had laid the groundwork for a belief in universal redemption, but had done so unintentionally.[51]

The intention of the preacher cannot always be the measuring rod for what the listener receives. As Haller has suggested, the "vitality of dogma is evinced as often in the heterodoxies it provokes as in the orthodoxy it maintains."[52] The Antinomians could win followers in the Army, not by telling the soldiers they were damned to everlasting perdition, but by telling them they were already saved—that they were saints of God. "We can now scarce speak with the vilest Drunkard, or Swearer, or covetous Worldling, or scorner at Godliness, but he hopes to be saved for all this," wrote Baxter:

> If you should go to all the Congregation, or Town, or Countrey, and ask them one by one, whether they hope to be saved? how few shall you meet with, that will not say yea? or that make any great question of it? But, O happy world, if Salvation were as common as this Hope![53]

When Saltmarsh wrote that faith was being persuaded more or less of Christ's love, he rendered himself vulnerable to Gatakers' derisive comment that any profane wretch might nourish such a persuasion *"more or les* upon groundles grounds. . . . *Who is there that have not* [such] *a desire?"*[54] Here is the explosive effect of Antinomian theology. All that any soldier of the Army needed to do to be freed from the burden of original sin which had been engraved upon his conscience by earlier teaching was to believe that he had become converted to Christ, to believe that he was now one of the saints. Inevitably, much of the intensive soul-searching and contemplation of Christ's divine nature and his merciful love that Saltmarsh said must accompany the act of believing would be swept aside. An Antinomian, wrote Francis Wortley, "hath found a shorter cut to heaven than the Catholicke Church ever heard of."[55]

The leading points of Antinomian theology now may be briefly summarized. They raise questions which will be considered in their political context in the succeeding chapters. Antinomian preachers rejected the contractual relationship between God and man of Federal Covenant theology. In the political realm it remains to be discovered whether or not this rejection meant a disbelief in a social contract between the ruler and the governed. In place of the Covenant theology the Antinomian preachers ascribed everything to the role of the indwelling Spirit or Free Grace in bringing salvation to the saints. The heavy emphasis on Free Grace among the chaplains raises the question of whether or not such a deterministic theology precluded a belief in political liberty. In the Antinomians' view all of the saints' sins were abolished without any acts of repentance or obedience; no expression of man's reason, will, or works was a condition of salvation. If this were so, how could a saint be sure that he was not confusing his faith, bestowed by the Free Grace of God's Spirit, with the individualistic voice of his own conscience or his own reason? Whether faith preceded or followed justification became a point of contention between the Antinomians and the Federalists. If faith followed justification, the saints possessed even greater certitude of salvation. Did this certitude of salvation mean that the saints could be identified and hence confidently granted political power? Although it says in the Antinomian doctrine that some are saved and some are damned, nevertheless men often behaved as if Christ were here and now in the breasts of all men. Was it possible that all were saved, and if so, should all participate politically in the life of the nation? Although Dell admitted in 1646 that the ranks of the saints were thin, he noted that the spiritual church had received a very great increase in the last few years, and further prophesied that it would finally grow in much larger numbers.[56] Whether it would grow sufficiently to include the entire nation—a kingdom of saints—was something that could only be left to the future revelations of the Holy Spirit.

CHAPTER THREE

Liberty of Conscience

In the mid-1640's the differences between the Antinomians and
Presbyterians over theology and religious worship were sorely
aggravated. Broadly speaking, the Antinomians held that men
could be saints or good men and yet not good Presbyterians;[1]
specifically, their main charge against Presbyterianism was that
it set up a religious uniformity which forced men to follow its
particular religious views. In a passage penned about the same
time as Milton's line "New Presbyter is but old Priest writ
large," Dell wrote "Presbyterian Uniformity, is neer a-kin to
Prelatical Conformity." The evil effect of Presbyterian uniformity could be seen, thought Dell, in the way it attempted to restrict the Spirit of God, which was not to be bound by any
coercive power of "poor, dark, ignorant, vain, foolish, proud,
and sinful men."[2] Christ alone, through the Holy Spirit, wrote
Collier, can overpower the soul and make men willing.[3] Church
magistrates were, therefore, not to interfere with the free operation of the Holy Spirit through Free Grace in men, i.e., with
Christian liberty. "Why is not free *Christian liberty*, peaceable
forbearance of each others *differing opinions*, and *practice* in
unity, more heard among us," wrote Saltmarsh, "and obedience,
conformity, and uniformity lesse?"[4] In this chapter we shall see
why a cry went up from the Antinomians for liberty of conscience, when at first glance it might appear that they, convinced of their own salvation before God, would be intolerant
of all others.

LIBERTY AND AUTHORITY

The doctrine of Christian liberty in Protestant thought has meant historically that the Gospel frees men *from* the burden of the Mosaic law and frees them *for* the service of God.[5] In a pamphlet published in November 1647, several ministers of London similarly defined the term:

> Christian liberty is not a wandering, and an unruly license, by the which we may doe, or leave undone whatsoever we list, at our pleasure: but it is a free gift bestowed upon us, by Christ our Lord, by the which the children of God (that is all the faithfull) being delivered from the curse of the law, or eternall death, and from the heavy yoake of the ceremoniall law, and being endowed with the holy ghost, beginne willingly of their own accord to serve God in holinesse and righteousnesse.[6]

The Antinomian chaplains concurred with the London ministers that freedom from the burden of the law did not mean license to indulge in sin, although they were frequently and unjustly attacked for allegedly condoning licentiousness. Abrogation of the law, they thought, did away with the coercive power of the church-state not only in ancient Israel but in contemporary Scotland as well. But did Christian liberty for these same chaplains imply liberty in the civil sphere also? Yes, was the emphatic answer of their hostile Presbyterian critic, Samuel Rutherford. He believed that there were "some peeping-up Antinomians in these daies, who said, their Christian liberty freed them from that yoake of subjection to lawfull Authority, Kings, Governours, Masters." But worse than that, wrote Rutherford, "Antinomians teach, that Saints should not serve, nor obey those that are not Saints, nor beleevers, as if Dominion and Civill power were found on grace, as Papists teach." When Dell wrote that all sins were annulled for those who truly believed, Rutherford said that if man could not sin against God, neither then could he sin against man. In other words, Rutherford did not believe that Christian liberty had purchased an exemption from obedience to human laws. Nevertheless, there is evidence that Rutherford's charge, as far as Saltmarsh was concerned, was partially true.[7]

Saltmarsh hoped that the example of God, loving men through the gift of the Spirit in His son Jesus Christ, would prevail upon the saints to love one another; this love, then, that believers bear for each other, would bring them an *outward* liberty in the sphere of nature. For example, when a man would "take hold of the *Skirt* of *him* that is a Jew [i.e., under the letter of the law] and say, we *heare that* God is in *you*," they would know that that man had ceased to love *only* his neighbor as the law of nature commanded but now loved his *enemy* as well as his neighbor according to the law of grace. They would know that he had raised himself from the love of worldly interests, and had disengaged himself from the love of power, riches, and earthly glory. Outward liberty was achieved by the believer to the degree to which nature was subsumed by grace; i.e., to that degree to which he had knowingly received the love of Christ into his own heart and had begun to manifest that love unto all other men. However, Saltmarsh did not think to use this statement of outward liberty as a wedge for greater political power.[8]

Saltmarsh's belief in religious liberty was crystallized as early as the Solemn League and Covenant of 1643. A clause in the New Model Ordinance of 15 February 1645 provided that all officers should take an oath to uphold the Covenant. Only Sir Ralph Verney in the Commons and John Lilburne in the Army refused to take it.[9] Peters stated that "he had take[n] it (as hee thought) at least twenty times, and saw nothing in it, that men should make such a stir about it."[10] In spite of this legislative action, the ambiguity of the Covenant occasioned a variety of interpretations from the most conscientious of the Antinomians. The Covenant enjoined men to preserve the Reformed religion of the Church of Scotland and to bring about the reformation of religion in England "according to the word of God and the example of the best reformed Churches." Because the church principle on which the ecclesiastical structure of the Presbyterian church was based was anathema to Saltmarsh, he subsequently interpreted the phrase "according to the word of God" to mean "so far as we doe or shall in our consciences conceive the same to be according to the word of God." This passage shows Saltmarsh's basic plea for liberty of conscience so that the Spirit (moving through Free Grace and not the power of men) could interpret the will of God. And Thomas Collier added that if religion is settled "according to the Word of God," no magistrate will settle it, for "none can bring [men] to true worship of God, but himselfe."[11]

In 1645 John Ley, a Presbyterian member of the Westminster Assembly, vigorously attacked Saltmarsh because of the chaplain's interpretation of the Solemn League and Covenant in terms of the individual conscience.[12] "You give up the Magistrates Authoritie to the peoples libertie, leaving it in their choice to receive, or refuse Church-government, as they like or dislike it," Ley admonished, "and what is this but to subject the Supreame Authority to the popular liberty?"[13] While Ley was afraid that "popular liberty" would know no bounds, Dell was afraid that "State freedom," as he called "popular liberty," would be crushed by the Presbyterians. Dell's beliefs on religious toleration grew in part out of his fear that Presbyterians aspired to political power. "It is no proper Presbyterial Doctrine, that does not (at least) meddle with the affairs of the State, which in time they may hopefully come to order." If the Presbyterians should control the state, Dell feared that they would "cunningly shrowd" the civil power of the state under the power of God. Such a doctrine, he maintained, would also deprive a man of his "State freedom," and to deprive a man of his "State freedom" for the sake of the kingdom of Christ was never ordained by the Gospel.[14]

What irked the chaplains the most about Presbyterianism, especially Presbyterian magistrates, was their attempt to reconcile religious differences by means of a Procrustean bed of religious conformity. Most unpalatable to the chaplains was the technique of "compulsive power" whereby the magistrate enforced through the civil law the doctrine and discipline of an established state church. Saltmarsh argued that whereas such a theocratic form of ecclesiastical polity had existed with divine sanction only in the kingdom of Israel of the Old Testament, it was now long since dissolved (as was the entire covenant of works) by the merciful grace of Christ.[15] Both Dell and Collier denied that the people of England or any nation could ever become the church of Christ; a nation cannot be a church. Instead, God "gathers" his church out of the elect, who have received a new birth through the "gift of the Spirit." Therefore, as John Webster stated so succinctly, *"not he whom man approveth, but he whom God approveth is justified."*[16]

By opposing the interference of the civil magistrate in religious affairs, the chaplains introduced an element of human responsibility into an otherwise deterministic theological scheme. Free will had no place in man's relation to God, as we have repeatedly seen, but the chaplains were prepared to defend to the last ounce of their blood the right, though they did not call it that, to be free from human manipulation in religious affairs. This ambivalent attitude toward free will can be clearly seen in Dell's attitude toward Erastianism. From Dell's point of view the danger to religious freedom came not only from the Presbyterians, but also from the Erastian lawyers, such as Prynne, who wanted Parliament to dominate the church. Prynne wrote that the conversion process, whereby the saints were turned from "sinful lusts" unto God, did not completely destroy the sin which stemmed from Adam; as a matter of fact, the saints might fall at any time into *"scandalous sinnes and capitall offences,"* though they would not fall totally from the state of grace. When this happened, said Prynne, the civil magistrate should interfere for the sinner's spiritual welfare as well as the good of the state. It was clear to Prynne that the corporal punishments of the civil magistrate "convert the inner man, soul, spirit, even morally and divinely, too, as well as the outward, and stop the current of mens sins."[17]

The measures Prynne recommended were pointless, according to Dell, since the souls of believers had already been inwardly reformed by the gift of the Holy Spirit. Prynne vindictively inquired:

> Will Mr. Dell . . . now proclaime to all the world in print . . . that none of all these workes of the flesh, No not Adultery, Fornication, uncleanesse, Idolatry, Witchcraft, Seditions, Heresies, Drunkenesse, Murder . . . are so much as once to be punished with any outward corporall or Capitall punishment whatsoever, by any Christian Magistrate, Master, Tutor, or Parent but only with the losse of heaven? Is this the Reformation that these *Newlights* intend? the *Liberty of Conscience* they preach for, write for, fight for?

Dell, on the contrary, as we have seen, wrote that "*Libertines* and *Licentious* persons" were to be restrained and punished by the civil magistrate whenever they transgressed in any matter *against their neighbor and against civil society.* Religious liberty did not mean freedom to indulge in licentiousness; but at the same time it did not mean state or Parliamentary control of the church or the religious consciences of men.[18]

But Prynne pushed the argument even further. If forcible reformation and violence are contrary to the Gospel, then surely taking up arms against the government is much more unlawful. Why is Mr. Dell a chaplain in the Army, asked Prynne, and why are so many of his saints men of blood and violence? The Army saints must renounce either their military employment or Dell's gospel of non-coercion. Apparently without hope for the latter alternative, Prynne pursued what he felt to be Dell's illogicality. Might not all the soldiers of Dell's "New-way" by "like or better Logick" conclude that since Christ came not to destroy men's lives but to save them, "*Ergo* we who are christian Soldiers (who must imitate our Capt. Jesus Christ) must now lay down our Armes, repent of all the blood [and] hence forth kill no more publike Enemies"? Dell was no pacifist. Whenever the saints clashed with coercing magistrates (Anglican or Presbyterian) over religious affairs, he took the position: "We ought to obey God, and not them."[19]

Further than this Dell would not go. He did, to be sure, write an occasional stirring passage, for example: "This is your heritage, O ye servants of the Lord, to make void the force of every weapon that is used against you, and to condemn every tongue that judgeth you."[20] But this rather vague assertion was not typical of the views of the Army preachers, or even of Dell himself, on the subject of resistance. Most of the Army preachers made it quite clear that they did not wish to make religion a stalking-horse for political ends. Collier, Denne, and Webster all insisted that religious liberty should in no way derogate from the just power of the magistrate in preserving the civil peace and liberty of the kingdom.[21] As Saltmarsh put it: "all *societies* and *Christians* by no *pretence* of *religion,* or liberty for the worship of God, are to *resist* or *disturb* the *civill administration.*" Liberty or indulgence for "tender consciences," he added, should not signify any diminution of the just power of the civil magistrate.[22] Dell concurred with Saltmarsh and the others on this point. He, too, argued that he did not understand the Church of Christ to be any "Company of Men whatsoever, who under the Notion of a Church of Saints, or any other Title, may plead Priviledge or exemption of their Lives, Liberties, or Estates, from the power of the Civil Magistrate." And as for setting up and exercising an outward, visible jurisdiction, such as Anglicanism or Presbyterianism, immune from the authority and power of the civil magistrate, it was "Anti-christian."[23]

If the Antinomian generally did not use Christian liberty as a means to plead exemption from civil laws, one might ask if the overwhelming power of God's grace in the act of redemption reduced his political role correspondingly to a cipher. As Cromwell put it in the Putney Debates: "We speak as men that desire to have the fear of God before our eyes, and men that may not resolve in the power of a fleshly strength to do that which we do, but to lay this as the foundation of all our actions, to do that which is the will of God."[24] This is a theme of Ernst Cassirer in his book *The Platonic Renaissance in England*. Cassirer felt that Hobbes and Puritanism were at political and religious antipodes, but on grounds of faith he thought they were in agreement. In both cases faith was subordinated to "an absolute will based on power." In Puritanism, wrote Cassirer, the power which cannot be resisted is the divine decree; in Hobbes the power which cannot be resisted is the law of the state.[25]

There is a passage in Dell's writing which seems to substantiate Cassirer's thesis. In his tract *Christ's Spirit*, Dell noticed a remarkable difference between grace and nature: "Nature, of one makes many; for we all . . . were but one in *Adam* . . . but Grace, of many makes one; for the Holy Spirit, which is as fire, melts all the Faithful into one mass or lump, and makes of many one Body, one thing, Yea it makes them one, in the Unity of God, according to that of Christ."[26] It has been pointed out that Hobbes has a very similar passage: "The only way to erect such a common power . . . is to conferre all their power and strength, and that way reduce all their wills, by plurality of Voices, into one will."[27] Hobbes's "one will" refers, of course, to the civil sphere and Dell's "one mass or lump" to the sphere of the spirit. Despite the fact that the chaplains constantly attributed everything to the Free Grace of God in salvation, and nothing to man's will, Dell believed: "Neither by making Christ all in the Kingdome of God, are you made ever the less in the kingdoms of this world."[28]

Fundamentally, as Cassirer says, Hobbes and the Antinomians were worlds apart. Puritanism asserted the claim of conscience and private judgment, Hobbes the preeminence of written law.[29] It was as champions of the individual conscience that the Antinomians made their contribution to political liberty.

UNITY AND UNIFORMITY

In opposition to the policy of compulsory "external Uniformity," which Dell called "the great *Diana* of the Presbyterians," he and Saltmarsh advocated a policy of voluntary inward unity. In this unity all men are taught of God and agree on the same truth (namely, there is one Lord, one faith, and one baptism) in accordance with their respective divine gifts.[30] It was clear to Dell that external uniformity did not exist in civil affairs. For example:

> Here in England you shall observe that *York* is not governed as *Hull,* nor *Hull* as *Hallifax* . . . there is no uniformity in the government of *Kent* and *Essex* . . . in *Godmanchester,* the youngest Son inherits, in *Huntington* the eldest . . . and yet between all Counties, Cities, Towns, Corporations, Companies, there is Unity, though no external Uniformity.[31]

If this is true in the civil state, asked Dell, why was it not all the more true in the visible churches of Christ's saints? While professing the need for unity, Dell, at the same time, regretted that such man-made terms as Presbyterian and Independent had grown up within the church. These terms, emphasizing the controversial outward forms of religion, he thought merely obfuscated the binding tie of all the saints—the uncontroversial inward presence of the Spirit of God. He disclaimed believing that any sect or religious group assuming the name of Anabaptist, Familist, Antinomian, Presbyterian, Socinian, Seeker, Independent, or any other name, had a monopoly on the saints of God.[32]

This emphasis on unity rather than uniformity was also precisely the sentiment of Oliver Cromwell as expressed in a letter to Speaker Lenthall from Bristol on 14 September 1645:

> Presbyterians, Independents, all had here the same spirit of faith and prayer; the same pretence and answer; they agree here, know no names of difference: pity it is it should be otherwise anywhere. All that believe, have the real unity, which is most glorious, because inward and spiritual, in the

Body, and to the Head. As for being united in forms, commonly called Uniformity, every Christian will for peace-sake study and do, as far as conscience will permit; and from brethren, in things of the mind we look for no compulsion, but that of light and reason.[33]

On the basis of such views as these on organized religion, which show an indifference to particular forms, Cromwell has been called a "spirituall anarchist" concerned with the principle of private judgment and spiritual freedom.[34] On the whole, this same indifference to particular ecclesiastical forms was characteristic of the chaplains. If, then, Cromwell and the chaplains regarded ecclesiastical uniformity as an unsatisfactory means for bringing religious peace to the kingdom, it remains to be seen what positive hope the chaplains held for ending the religious strife by arguing for the unity of theological belief.

The basic premise of Dell and Saltmarsh with respect to church government was that the outward form of worship must proceed from the inward belief. The visible church on earth, according to Saltmarsh, was to be made up of the "true, reall, essentially spirituall living stones" called saints, and this visible church was to be patterned after the invisible or mystical church above. But these stones, those who visibly, formally, and outwardly appeared to be saints, differed in degree and kind just as the stars differed. Some of these precious stones were sapphires; others were agates. Despite this variety in the treasure-trove of Christ, it must not be forgotten that the saints all enjoyed Christian liberty, which freed them from the bondage of sin and the burdensome obligations of the Mosaic law. The saints were now free to believe the truth as revealed through the word of God in the Scriptures and through the Spirit of Christ, which appeared as a light within their hearts. The practical problem involved here was whether the truth or light rested in the Presbyterians, in the Independents, in the Anabaptists, or in the Seekers. Saltmarsh's answer was that some fragment of truth was contained in all of these groups. Someone sees one thing for the truth; someone else sees another thing for the truth; and all see something short of the fullness of truth.[35]

The fragmentary nature of truth Saltmarsh and Dell both compared to the journey of travelers to the city of London. Just as there are many roads to Rome, so do men travel to the capital of the English realm from the north, south, east, and west. Each city-bound wayfarer has a portion of the truth; for example, the Independents have a purer communion of saints than the others, the Anabaptists have a baptism modeled after the Apostles, the Seekers are distinctive because they are looking for their church ordinances by the first pattern of the word of God, and the Presbyterians have a principle of administration (just what it was Saltmarsh never indicated) which may help the commonwealth or Parliament. Therefore, because each man has a contribution to make in erecting the full structure of truth, "Let us not . . . assume any power of *infallibility* to each other . . . for anothers *evidence* is as dark to me as mine to his . . . till the *Lord* enlighten us both for *discerning* alike."[36]

Clearly convinced of each man's fallibility in perceiving the whole truth, Saltmarsh proceeded to outline a program whereby these four religious groups might cease assailing one another's religious beliefs. In a tract published in 1646, he urged, as Dell and Cromwell had done, that the names of all sects and divisions should be laid aside. In addition, he asked that freedom of the press be granted all those who were not allowed pulpits for preaching. Finally, along with Peters, he advocated free debates and open conferences in order to settle differences in spiritual matters. The most one can do, according to Saltmarsh, is to say: Here is a form of church government *"which to some of us seemeth to be a Government according to the Word; take it and examine it: if you be so perswaded . . . embrace it; if not, do not obey any thing in* blind *and* implicit *obedience."* Earlier Saltmarsh had warned that it was wrong to judge error or heresy as those who are "pentioners to the multitude" do, that is by measuring it "by those that are for it, or against it."[37]

Dell was also an advocate of free speech and a free press. He argued that if men were not allowed to vent their religious views publicly without reprisal, they would spread them privately and thus would infect and corrupt many with their errors. The only right way to conquer error was with the truth. Man's truth, of course, was only a partial truth, whereby error was to be tested, because the smoke was still in the temple and the angels still pouring out their vials; no one man had yet attained full truth. All the saints will in the end meet in one glorious truth, wrote Collier, but anyone who presumes to have this truth now and on this ground suppresses opinions, sets himself "in the roome of God" and acts out of "grosse ignorance" and "desperate pride."[38]

The author of the most famous plea for the freedom of the press in that age possessed views that were in some respects closely akin to those of Saltmarsh and Dell. Milton wrote of truth in the *Areopagitica* as if it were another name for virtue; in the knowledge of truth he saw the principal sign of salvation and the prime qualification for political rule. Wisdom, Milton contended, could only be achieved through the exercise of reason, and reason was the choosing between good and evil. But to choose wisely one had to know all the alternatives, for in the final analysis good could be known only through the knowledge of evil. Indeed, even though a man's belief be true, yet unless it had been subjected to error, "the very truth he held became his heresy": "He that can apprehend and consider vice with all her baits and seeming pleasures, and yet abstain, and yet distinguish, and yet prefer that which is truly better, he is the true wayfaring Christian." Because "a fugitive and cloistered virtue" cannot attain the "immortal garland" until it is tried in combat, it is necessary to read all kinds of tracts and to hear all kinds of reasoning. Freedom for all books and ideas, whether good or evil, is imperative so that they can be laid before the altar of reason from which the truth can be ascertained.[39]

As for truth itself, Milton held that it was an absolute body of knowledge which originally came into the world without deformity in any particular. But a "wicked race of deceivers . . . hewd her lovely form into a thousand pieces," leaving her friends the job of piecing her back together again.[40] This slow task has been the work of both ancient writers and members of the true religion, for such a "closing up [of] truth to truth" is the golden rule of theology; it cannot be completed, however, until the second coming of Christ, at which time truth will be molded into an "immortall feature of loveliness and perfection." Until the second coming, Milton admonished men not to allow the prohibitions of the civil magistrate to stand in the way of the seekers of truth. All religious sects must be tolerated, for each in its own way is contributing toward that great truth— the temple of the Lord—that all men are erecting together. The difference between them is that some cut the marble whereas others hew cedars, and the relationship of one to another is not continuity but rather contiguity: "Nay rather the perfection consists in this, that out of many moderat varieties and brotherly dissimilitudes that are not vastly disproportionall, arises the goodly and the gracefull symmetry that commends the whole pile and structure." Since there was an indestructible reason implicit in all men, dulled by the Fall, but ever seeking a new brightness, it was clear that no minister, no Westminster divine, no King, could legitimately restrict the freedom of the human mind in religious matters.[41]

Milton held that it was possible for all men to become believers if they would but choose the true religion, if they would accept Scripture, interpreted by the individual conscience under the guidance of the Holy Spirit, as the sole authority between man and God. And what if there were differences among men in the interpretation of Scripture? Indeed, Milton himself held beliefs that seemed heretical to others: for example, his ideas regarding divorce. Milton faced the issue squarely when he wrote in *Christian Doctrine*: "If . . . there be any difference among professed believers as to the sense of

Scripture, it is their duty to tolerate such difference in each
other, until God shall have revealed the truth to all."[42] This was
Dell's solution as well. If men cannot agree, he wrote, let them
follow St. Paul's rule and leave the final judgment of the matters
in question to the due time appointed by God.[43]

The urgency of political matters, however, did not always
leave time for new revelations of truth from God. This dilemma
was dramatized at the Army Debates at Putney in October and
November, 1647. An impasse had been reached in the debate
between the Levellers and Ireton (aided by Cromwell) on
what was to be done with the King and the House of Lords.
During the debate both Cromwell and Lieutenant Colonel
Goffe urged the participants in their differences to hearken to
the voice of God speaking to their consciences, for " 'tis God
that persuades the heart." To speak in the name of the Lord,
said Cromwell, meant ultimately to speak according to your
conscience. But as men with the conviction of the Spirit of God
speak, he continued, contradictions appear, and have appeared.[44] For example, as we have seen, Ireton had contended
that only those with a "permanent fixed interest" in the kingdom, the forty-shilling freeholders, should be given the right
to vote, and Rainborough had replied that the poorest man in
England had a life to live just as the greatest man. Which man
spoke for God? Cromwell met this problem by attempting to
minimize the differences between the parties; they differed only
over means, he declared, not ends. For instance, all agreed that
the King and the Lords were dangerous to the nation; there was
disagreement only when it came to particulars, such as whether
the King and Lords should be preserved or destroyed. Earlier,
Cromwell had observed that difficulties could be answered by
faith, but he wisely added that all men are apt to call that faith
which might only be "carnal imagination, and carnal reasonings." As Captain [John] Clarke put it: "We shall find that we
have submitted the Spirit of God unto the candle of reason,
whereas reason should have been subservient unto the Spirit of

God." Nature and grace through reason and the Holy Spirit had become inextricably entangled in the human conscience.[45]

How was the Spirit of God to be separated from the chaff of human reason in honest men? And how, for that matter, could dishonest men be prevented from using religious meetings as a front for their designs and insinuations? Dell answered these questions by suggesting that the saints must labor to distinguish between gifts natural to man and gifts that flowed from God's Spirit.[46] Cromwell's answer was simply: "Let the rest judge!" But this was no decision to be made by majority votes. When the evidence is not clear, said Cromwell, the best way to judge a matter is by whether or not it conforms with the law written in us, the Spirit of God; given enough time, this Spirit will certainly prevail, since further extraordinary manifestations of it have been promised by God. Even Cromwell realized, however, that there must be some outward evidence to test the actual presence of the Holy Spirit. He seized upon John Jubbes's statement that the signs of the Spirit of God were to be found in meekness, gentleness, mercy, patience, forbearance, and love. These were hardly the characteristics of the man who within a year and a half was to bring Charles I to trial for his life, and as we might expect, Cromwell had his reservations:

> I think that he that would decline the doing of justice where there is no place for mercy, and the exercise of the ways of force, for the safety of the kingdom, where there is no other way to save it, and would decline these out of the apprehensions of danger and difficulties in it, he that leads that way . . . doth [truly] lead us from the law of the Spirit of life, the law written in our hearts.

John Wildman, the Leveller, said that he, too, wanted to reverence the Spirit of God, and could do so with confidence in spiritual matters, for which the Scriptures served as an authoritative guide. Civil matters were something else again: "We cannot find anything in the word of God [of] what is fit to be done in civil matters."[47]

Cromwell's communion with the Spirit of God led him to political views based upon custom and privilege, Wildman's to the doctrine of natural rights and majority rule. By appealing to the voice of the Spirit of the Lord, men could justify highly individualistic and frequently incompatible political points of view.

The Antinomian appeal to the Holy Spirit for guidance in earthly affairs was made by many of those present at the Putney Debates. What the participants sought was not the outward compulsive uniformity of religious or political forms but the inward voluntary unity of God's truth, upon which, it was hoped, they would all be able to agree. They were fully aware that God's full truth as yet had not been clearly revealed; they realized that they must attempt to arrive at an approximation of the truth (God's plan for England) through debate and discussion. In doing this they rendered a fundamental service to the democratic process.

But free debate was one thing, majority votes another, and it was here that the Army preachers drew the line. They were willing to submit their spiritual and political views to free debates, but they were no more eager than Cromwell to put these views at the mercy of a majority vote. The debate at Putney was essentially an attempt to introduce spiritual values, derived from God and as yet imperfectly apprehended only by the saints, into a realm of political values created by men. Whereas the Leveller, Wildman, wished to allow the majority of all men to determine political values, Cromwell was content to rely upon the few. It will become even more apparent in the following pages that the Army preachers felt the same way.

Grace and Nature

Was religious liberty to be extended equally to all men, or only to a prescribed number? Are we justified, Saltmarsh asked, because there are many different opinions and interpretations about salvation, in saying that all in all ways can be saved, every man believing what he wishes? His answer to his own question was an emphatic No. Such a solution is one way to make peace, wrote Saltmarsh, but not the right way, for it denies the unity of belief that all men should agree upon. Dell, too, although he would not allow civil action in religious matters, was perfectly willing to allow the true church, in cases where the retention of points of doctrine would mean "unavoidable damnation," to condemn the doctrine and to excommunicate the persons involved.[1] But the liberty of conscience that the churches approve is one thing; the degree of toleration that the state will allow is another.

The charge of "universal toleration" was frequently leveled against the Army preachers. For instance, when Peters wrote that "all children shall be fed, though they have several faces and shapes," Nathaniel Ward replied that whereas he himself was for a Christian forbearance toward those that differed on religious issues, his forbearance extended only to "circumstan-tiall" differences, i.e., differences which did not destroy the foundations of faith:

> But to go as far as you do, that all children of severall faces and shapes must be fed, that is in plain English, that all men though of severall judgments and opinions must be toller-ated, this I utterly renounce as unwarranted by Scripture,

and inconsistent with the peace of the Church, or safety of the Commonwealth."[2]

Dell, too, recognized that there were some points of doctrine so fundamental that, as Roger Williams put it, "without right belief thereof a man cannot be saved,"[3] but he felt that men who disputed even these points could safely be tolerated:

> Now in case the Doctrine, wherein we differ, be such as is absolutely necessary to Salvation, and without believing which, men can have no interest in Christ, yet even in this Case . . . Hear them speak, and be rather confident, that the truth of God will prevail over their error, than fearful, that their error will prevail against the truth; and so strive not for Secular Power, to shut up mens mouths, and to restrain mens writings, though they speak and print things that seem never so contrary to the truth of God, and Doctrine of the Gospel.[4]

Dell preached that it was wrong for a minister of the gospel to ask a secular magistrate for power to punish a dissenter, or imprison him, or sell his goods, "as is now practiced in some parts of the Kingdom, even upon the Saints." There should be no civil restrictions upon the voluntary gathering of the invisible church of the spiritual elect.[5] But Christopher Love was quick to reply: "What is this but to say . . . that the Magistrate should give an universall Toleration to any one who will call themselves Saints . . . could you . . . inforce this, you would put a weapon into the hands of Papisticall, Prelaticall, Anabaptisticall, Anarchicall and Malignant men."[6]

In 1644 Saltmarsh had been greatly annoyed with the term "universal toleration" just as he had been annoyed also with "universal salvation." He would not accept the position of universal toleration because, basically, it allowed heathens and Papists, those who could not agree on the unity of belief, to enjoy liberty of conscience. "A truth I conceive may be no more *suppressed ignorantly*," wrote Saltmarsh, "then it may be *persecuted ignorantly*." The persecution of truth ignorantly, which was Williams' fear, is not as dangerous an evil, said Saltmarsh, as allowing the unity of belief (truth) to be suppressed by views which are clearly false. To allow all to "propagate their interests equally with that, which is the commonly received truth" results in a moratorium on truth. In 1646, however, Saltmarsh wrote as if he believed in the very concept he had previously denounced.

> When *Christians* are under several *forms* and *administrations*, and these diametrical, or opposite to each other, and mutually *contradicting* and *expelling* each other, here can be no Peace nor Preservation of all, but from an indulgency or liberty in all; and this is such a liberty as *men* may give to *men*; this is the liberty of the *outward* man.

It is no wonder, then, that the chaplains' views on religious toleration led, at least from the point of view of their critics, to a general belief in toleration for all men. To Saltmarsh the question was whether or not there must be a "plenary liberty," i.e., whether or not all must be tolerated "for fear of persecuting the truth through ignorance." The answer ultimately became clear to him: there was no guaranteeing religious liberty to the saints without guaranteeing religious liberty to all men.[7] Upon this argument, wrote A. S. P. Woodhouse, depends the direct contribution of Puritanism to general liberty.[8]

SEPARATION OF CHURCH AND STATE

Contrary to the teachings of John Cotton that the field in which the wheat was sown was the church and that the tares were hypocrites within the church, Roger Williams believed that the field is the world or civil state.[9] The good seed or the wheat that is sown in the field is the children of God or the elect, and the tares are the children of evil or the unregenerate.[10] There is no need to root out the tares (persecute the unregenerate), since they will be burned at the final harvest, the Lord being fully capable of making the necessary distinctions without the assistance of civil magistrates.[11] Indeed it is useless for the magistrates to try to save the unregenerate from sin, because that would be an admission of that "Arminian, popish doctrine of freewill, as if it lay in their own power and ability to believe upon the magistrate's command."[12] Moreover, one might easily mistake wheat for tares.

Williams, therefore, advocated religious toleration for all men. Such a theory seemed all the more necessary to Williams because he believed the chosen of God might be found in pagan or anti-Christian religions as well. His concern was with *all* the elect; hence his idea of a delaying action (by necessity extended to all men) until such time as God (who alone knows who the elect are) separates the tares from the wheat. Toleration was, then, but one part of the program for saving the elect out of the "lamentable shipwreck of mankind."[13] That is why he had to adopt the radical step of divorcing grace from nature, for in no other way could the elect follow God's apocalyptic itinerary with a reasonable amount of ease.

What few allusions to the parable of the tares and the wheat the chaplains made showed them to be in agreement with Williams on the danger of mistaking wheat for tares.[14] They agreed also in restricting the role of the state in religious questions to that of a "nursing father" who allows the religion of the spirit to flourish and does not interfere with it.[15] Thus Saltmarsh and Dell were faced with the same practical dilemma as Roger Williams: what to do about a theocratic polity supported by a close alliance of the spiritual and civil magistracy? These overlapping prerogatives of the world of nature and the world of grace produced the matrix in the seventeenth century from which ideas of religious toleration were born.

In order to achieve universal toleration, Williams proposed the complete separation of the spheres of influence of church and state.

> The church . . . is like unto . . . a corporation, society, or company of East India or Turkey merchants or any society or company in London: which hold disputations, and in

matters concerning their society may dissent, divide, break into schisms and factions, sue and implead each other at the law, yea, wholly break up and dissolve into pieces and nothing, and yet the peace of the city not be in the least measure impaired or disturbed; because the essence or being of the city, and so the well being and peace thereof is essentially distinct from these particular societies.[16]

This idea, which Woodhouse has called the principle of segregation, has the effect not only of spiritualizing the church (be it visible or invisible), but of secularizing the state as well.[17] It repeatedly seeks expression in Williams' two major works, *The Bloudy Tenent of Persecution* (1644) and its companion tract, *The Bloudy Tenent Yet More Bloudy* (1652), which were written during his two brief visits to England. It means the complete rejection of the national chuch concept, be it Anglican or Presbyterian, and states that all people—Jews, Papists, Turks, Arminians, Anabaptists, or anti-Christians—should have the opportunity to worship God as they pleased without persecution from the civil magistrates. Williams had suffered banishment from the Boston theocracy. He was determined to attack at every opportunity its Genevan model of church government.

Saltmarsh's and Dell's resolution of the problem of theocratic polity was similar to Williams'. "The *kingdom* of *Christ* and the *world* are *two*," wrote Saltmarsh, "in their *fundamentalls, policy, Laws, governours, ends, designes.*"[18] The kingdom of Christ was to be ruled by the law of grace, the civil state by the law of nature:

> Nature lives by this law, preserve thy *self*, thy *life*, thy *lands*, thy *rights* and *priviledges, avenge* thy self, *an eye for an eye, and a tooth for a tooth*, and love only thy neighbor: *Grace* lives by this *law*, deny *thy self*, forsake *lands, life, houses*, take up *the Cross*, if he take *thy cloak let him have thy coat also*, love *thy enemies*, bless *them that curse thee*; when *thou art reviled revile not again, when thou suffer'st threaten not.*[19]

The province of nature was the civil state; the ruler was the magistrate, whose function was to distinguish between good and evil according to the dictates of right reason. The province of grace was the church; the ruler was Christ as revealed in the Spirit, and the Spirit was to express the truth while preventing heresy.[20]

However, Saltmarsh did not precisely indicate where the borderline lay between truth and goodness or between heresy and evil. Antinomian millenarianism, which will be discussed in the next chapter, tended to blot out these differences. In separating nature and grace, the state and the church, Dell and Saltmarsh worked to spiritualize the church but, instead of secularizing the state, they strove to spiritualize it also. Neither urged that Jews, Catholics, and non-Christians be tolerated; rather, it seems clear that their toleration does not extend beyond the unity of belief which only the saints, including the Presbyterians, have, and which Catholics and Jews can never possibly agree upon. The scope of the toleration which the Antinomians were demanding from the prevailing Presbyterianism therefore stood little chance of being enlarged by the saints' accession to power.

Williams did not confine his political views to the separation of church and state. In the most significant political passage of all his writing, Williams placed sovereignty directly in the hands of the people, subject only to the restrictions of natural law:

> But from this grant I infer, as before hath been touched, that the sovereign, original, and foundation of civil power, lies in the people—whom they must needs mean by the civil power distinct from the government set up: and if so, that a people may erect and establish what form of government seems to them most meet for their civil condition. It is evident that such governments as are by them erected and established, have no more power, nor for no longer time, than the civil power, or people consenting and agreeing, shall betrust them with. This is clear not only in reason, but in the ex-

perience of all commonweals, where the people are not deprived of their natural freedom by the power of tyrants.[21]

In short, the people are the sovereign civil power, they may erect whatever polity they choose, and governments have only as much power as the people delegate to them (a covenant theory). The chaplains' views on these three points will be considered in the following pages.

Williams was not particularly concerned with which particular form the government should take: "Whether that form is monarchical, aristocratic, democratic, or what-not, is of little consequence so long as it serves its citizens." Because Williams conceived of civil constitutions as the ordinances of men, he believed that government must be adapted to the different natures and dispositions of the peoples of the world, and that it was unlawful for one nation to question another's government and laws. Yet he left little doubt that his personal choice was for a democratic form of government. This is made clear in the following quotation from the charter of 1644 for the colony of Rhode Island which Williams obtained during his first return visit to England:

> It is agreed, by this present Assembly thus incorporate, and by this present act declared, that the form of Government established in Providence Plantations is Democratical; that is to say, a Government held by the free and Voluntary consent of all, or the greater part of the free inhabitants.

In this and similar documents the democratic political theories of Roger Williams were embodied in the historical records of the colony of Rhode Island.[22]

In seeking the explanation for Williams' political views, Woodhouse was impelled to consider whether or not politics can be influenced by (or in turn influence) religion if grace and nature are in distinct spheres. His answer was clearly in the affirmative; the means of influence was the principle of analogy. We shall give special attention to this analogical reasoning in the following analysis of the relationship of religion and politics in three categories: equality and sainthood, covenant and grace, and elective polity and anarchy.

On equality, analogical reasoning states the principle as follows: "As in the order of grace all believers are equal, so in the order of nature all men are equal; as the church is composed of believers all equally privileged, so the state should be composed of men all equally privileged."[23] Hence, the equality of believers in Christ must logically lead to the equality of men in civil affairs. The Antinomian chaplains, especially Dell, certainly insisted upon the equality of believers in Christ. No man is higher or lower than another in the kingdom of God, wrote Dell; land, money, learning, and titles of nobility were no prerequisites for sainthood. It was every bit as easy for a poor "mechanick" to become persuaded of Christ's love through the Holy Spirit as it was for a nobleman or a king. However, the equality of believers in grace, according to Dell, did not have a counterpart in the world of nature:

> For though according to our first Nativity, whereby we are born of men, there is great inequality, some being born high, some low, some honourable, some mean, some *Kings*, some *Subjects*, &c. yet according to our new or second birth, whereby we are born of God, there is exact equality; for here are none better or worse, higher or lower, but all have the same faith, hope, love.[24]

The weakness of analogical reasoning with respect to equality is that it makes no provision (either in the world of grace or in the world of nature) for the non-believers, the non-elect, the lost souls arbitrarily assigned to eternal perdition. By definition they are not in the sphere of grace and cannot be transferred by analogy into the civil sphere along with the elect, the saints of God. To do this a society of great *inequality* rather than equality would be formed. The civil state would then consist of two classes—the rulers and the ruled, the saints and the godless.

A strict interpretation of the theology of the chaplains precluded their believing in universal salvation although, as exponents of Free Grace, they were accused of this belief. "I know not how it comes to passe, but so it is," wrote John Owen, "men . . . make free grace, that glorious expression, to be nothing but that which is held forth in this their opinion, *viz.* that God loveth *all,* and gave Christ to dye for *all,* and is ready to save *all,* if they will come to *him.*"[25] Such a man was the Leveller William Walwyn, who admitted in 1649 that he had long before espoused the doctrine "(called then, Antinomian) of free justification by Christ alone." But Walwyn's theology, as Haller has noted, was a very loose interpretation of Antinomianism. It was humanistic and non-mystical, and never became involved in theological disputation. Nevertheless, it is somewhat surprising to find Walwyn stating in *A Whisper in the Eare:* "I am one that do truly and heartily love all mankind, it being the unfeigned desire of my soul, that all men might be saved." As an Antinomian Walwyn believed in equality of rights before the political bar of justice. Only Walwyn, however, among the prominent Levellers, was attracted to Antinomianism.[26]

Woodhouse has suggested that Arminianism, by breaking down the arbitrary boundaries between the children of light and the children of darkness, undermined one of the strongest barriers between Puritanism and democracy.[27] This statement assumes that Arminianism, by emphasizing man's free will, fostered a belief in universal salvation. Although the five points set forth in 1610 by the Remonstrants, who were followers of Arminius, did not state this doctrine, it was nevertheless commonly imputed to their successors. "Arminians," said Samuel Rutherford, "fight for free will, and universal atonement, and generall Redemption, of all and every one."[28]

Yet one must be cautious on generalizations about Arminianism and equality. John Lilburne, the chief Leveller, never committed himself to Arminianism, and John Milton, an Arminian in theology, preached not political equalitarianism but a civil aristocracy of virtue. It seems that the Leveller idea of equality owes as much, if not more, to a philosophy of natural rights as it does to religious doctrine.[29] The equality of the Army preachers, as Ernest Troeltsch said of the Pauline ethic, is primarily an equality of saints before God but not before man.

COVENANT AND GRACE

Still another means by which Woodhouse's thesis might be validated came from the idea of the covenant. It found expression in two ways, the one ecclesiastical, the other theological. The solemn oath or covenant taken by the Congregational church to walk in the ways of God provided by analogy the ecclesiastical model for the social contract. The classic instance of this is the Mayflower Compact.[30] Not only Congregationalists in New England but Presbyterians in Scotland and England, also addicted to the idea of the church covenant, were able to develop political covenants—the two most famous being the Scottish National Covenant of 1638 and the Solemn League and Covenant in 1643.[31] The theological covenant between God and man (*"I will be your God, and ye shall be my people"*), about which the Presbyterian Rutherford wrote in his tract *Lex, Rex*, also had its counterpart in the political realm. Rutherford described in addition a covenant between a king and his people, which gave a claim to the people against a king who, seduced by wicked counsel, made war upon the land.[32]

Even Baxter, who was imbued with Covenant theology, very briefly noted in his autobiography his great attraction in the 1640's to the politics of George Lawson, a pre-Lockean advocate of the concept of political trusteeship, the separation of powers, and the importance of a remedial power, upon the dissolution of an old government, to erect a new government.[33] And, to be sure, one may find most of these concepts, including the idea of the covenant, in Baxter's political writings, especially his *Holy Commonwealth*. However, his idea of the covenant must be understood in the context of his basic political presupposition, namely, that the best government is not a democracy—"I like not the Democratick formes"—but instead a theocratic or divine commonwealth in which God, not the people, was sovereign. What he was most interested in securing for the commonwealth, as he stated in his "Preface," was a "succession of wise and godly men"—the saints—as political rulers. Although the saints were to rule over a commonwealth which would have a separate administration from the church, nevertheless Baxter believed that the church and the commonwealth should be almost the same—hence a theocratic polity. "But that which I mean," he wrote, "is, that the same qualification maketh a man capable of being a member both of a Christian Church and Commonwealth, which is, his Covenant with God in Christ, or his Membership of the Universal Church." In other words, in Baxter's idea of the covenant, the same persons, the godly, are fit to be members of both the church and the commonwealth. Theocratic polity in this way, then, brings about the "unquestionable reign of Christ on earth." The political manifestations of Covenant theology as exemplified in Baxter's *Holy Commonwealth* suggest the outward forms of the Lockean social contract; however, the inward substance, as Richard Schlatter suggests, is a theocratic polity emphasizing government by good men rather than by good laws.[34]

The Antinomian chaplains held neither to covenanting among members of particular congregations nor to convenanting between man and God. There is no suggestion of a social contract in their thought. It is true that Peters early in his career in Holland committed himself to the idea of a church covenant[35] and during his stay in New England, at least, was an adherent of Covenant theology, but he was no spokesman for the social contract. Perhaps Peters' close association in the New Model Army with his colleagues Dell and Saltmarsh had allowed him to assimilate some of the ideas of the Antinomians.[36] Like Baxter, though from different theological premises, the Army chaplains came to believe, as we shall see, in government by the saints.

ELECTIVE POLITY AND ANARCHY

Although Dell considered the laws of grace and the laws of nature to be wholly separate, he found some close similarities between them. Just as he compared the political unity of Hull and Halifax with the ecclesiastical unity of Presbyterianism and Independency, so also he compared the saints' right to congregate with the rights of people in free societies. "For if every free Society hath power to chuse its own Officers, much more hath the true Church this power; being (as is said) the freest Society under Heaven." Moreover, as those who appoint evil officers in civil societies have the power to remove them, so also the church has the same power.[37] Dell's premises are Leveller doctrine—popular election and removal of civil magistrates.

John Bastwick, a Presbyterian, proceeding like Dell by analogy from nature to grace, reaches a very different conclusion: "And as it is in the affaires secular and in the State, so it is in the affaires of the Church, those in authority in the Church are to mannage the affaires and businesses of the Church and not the people." Saltmarsh, who was not attracted to the principle of analogy ("It is not safe going to the *State* for a *Paterne* for the Church"), seriously doubted "whether in *spirituals*, as in *Civils*, Votes and Voyces are to make Laws." Divine laws are made without the vote of any man, wrote Saltmarsh, and that should be a law or a truth in the church or the kingdom of saints which has the "Gospell-truth" in it, "not what is so in the common *consent* or *voyce*."[38]

Another chaplain, William Erbury, remarked that the spheres of grace and nature each offered three different kinds of government: monarchy, aristocracy, and democracy. In civil terms, these forms correspond to government by the King, by Parliament, and by the people. Church government has taken analogous forms:

Well, the Churches must have power and rule also, the Prelatick Church was *Monarchical*, all were ruled by one, by an Archbishop, the Kingly power of Prerogative fell by that:

the Presbyterian Church is an *Aristocracy,* the Elders or chief of these govern as 'twere in a Parliament, and Parliamentary Priviledges was like to fall by them; if not fallen already. The Independent or baptized Churches (both is one) are a pure *Democracy,* for not the ruling men or Ministers, but all the members, have equall power to order and ordain as they professe; and therefore called Independent. I wish they were so.

Erbury concluded by saying that in England all three forms had fallen to the saints "who see God in Spirit" and for whom "the Churches are nothing."[39]

Sir Charles Firth was one who believed that the ecclesiastical theories of the Independents, when applied to politics, developed into the fundamental principles of democratic government.[40] Considerable difficulty with this thesis arises when it is applied to the New Model Army during our period. On the whole, there is little or no evidence that the eccleciastical life of the soldiers from 1645 to 1647 was organized along the lines of a voluntary or self-governing church, or indeed, for that matter, in accordance with *any* form of church polity after the Presbyterian chaplains left. Richard Baxter, as we have seen, had been invited to form Oliver Cromwell's troop into a "gathered church" several years before the New Model was formed. The picture one might get of each company, troop, regiment, or brigade so organized did not materialize because the small number of chaplains who served the Army in 1645–47 usually were assigned not to individual units but to the staff of the Army. But more important, the chaplains, for the most part, were not partisans of visible forms of church government. Like Cromwell, they were "Spiritual anarchists." Such an attitude was hardly conducive to successful civil government.

Yet even if the chaplains had been devotees of the "gathered church" concept, such ecclesiastical practices would have proved quite incompatible with the hierarchy and rigid military discipline of army life. John Ley saw the incongruity with considerable insight. If an army is made up of self-governing congregations,

> Every Captaine and his company are free to attempt, or act, as they can agree among themselves, without subordination to superior Commander; if so, the Army would not be an Army, that is, an entire and well compacted systeme, or body of souldiers united, and regulated by prudence, and authoritie in a graduall series of Martiall command and government, but would breake in pieces into petty parties, as it is upon a rout made by the enemy, and so would be of little use, or force, either for conflict, or conquest, much lesse would it be terrible as *an armie with banners* should be.[41]

Even if self-governing congregations had existed in the Army, such dissident communions of saints could develop only with difficulty into Lilburne's "all-inclusive" community of citizens.[42]

With few exceptions, the chaplains did not advocate equality in the civil sphere because they did not believe in universal salvation. They adhered to no social contract because their belief in Free Grace made no provision for theological or ecclesiastical covenants. They did not, for the most part, develop specific forms of political government because they did not believe in specific forms of church government. The complete separation of nature and grace, so essential for the operation of the principle of analogy, was broken down, as we shall see, by the countervailing millenarian views of the chaplains, which led them more often than not in the direction of authoritarian government by the sanctified few.

C H A P T E R   F I V E

Right and Might Well Met

In the preceding chapter we examined the first member of the politico-religious polarity which I have designated as separatism and millenarianism; in this chapter we shall consider the second member. Millenarianism, as we shall see, had some strong affinities with the idea of power among the Army's preachers.

MILLENARIANISM

Francis Wortley defined an Antinomian as one who "talkes much of a new began Kingdom of Christ, set up in the hearts and soules of the Saints, which dischargeth him of all Secular duty. He is confident, that this is that Kingdome of Glory here, which shall last a thousand yeeres, and expects no other."[1] Most of the Army preachers as well as Oliver Cromwell seemed to envision human history as moving toward a final establishment of the kingdom of Christ upon earth. Saltmarsh, for example, wrote of the three ages of the world: law, grace, and the forthcoming age of the spirit; for Erbury the three dispensations were the law, the gospel, and Christ. "The best of us," wrote Erbury, "fancy a reign of Christ on earth for a thousand years, and the Saints to reign with him."[2]

In the terminology of Reinhold Niebuhr, most of the chaplains were what might be called "suffering," as opposed to "fighting," saints. Saltmarsh, Erbury, Dell, and Collier, for example, believing that the kingdom of Christ would be ushered in through the progressive revelation of God in the Spirit to individual men, simply awaited the millennium and speculated on the time of its advent (Dell held that his contemporaries would not live to see it, Saltmarsh that "the dawnings of light" might come very shortly). The "fighting" saints, by contrast, were ready for direct action, ready to bind their kings in chains and fetter their nobles with links of iron. "The work of God will go on," said Peters at the Putney Debates, but "I am not in the mind we should put our hands in our pockets and wait what will come."[3]

Most of the chaplains and Cromwell at first believed that the kingdom of Christ was only a spiritual and not a literal kingdom.[4] To Saltmarsh and Collier it was not something new but only a higher manifestation of the Holy Spirit already in the saints.[5] Saltmarsh firmly believed that any conception of Christ's reign or kingdom was occasioned by "the *Allegories*, and *Allusions*, and *Parables* the *Spirit* speaks; which they that are weak and carnal . . . take more in the *Letter* then in the *Spirit*."[6] Dell wrote in 1646 that the kingdom of God is not a "Temporal, or an Ecclesiastical Dominion, but a Spiritual."[7] Erbury, too, was convinced that Christ, reigning with his saints, would judge and govern the kingdoms and nations of this world, "but this Monarchical Government of Christ, and the Saints of the most high with him will not be in worldly Government and glory."[8]

How can these millenarian views be reconciled with the chaplains' separation of grace and nature? Dell, as we have seen, argued in 1646 that you cannot deprive a man of his state freedom for the sake of the kingdom of Christ, and in general had feared that Presbyterianism would shroud civil power under the power of God. If this was true of Presbyterianism, was it not true of other religious groups, too? After 1648 Dell left the impression that he separated grace and nature more to keep the church (or kingdom of Christ) free from meddling by the civil magistrate than to keep the saints out of political affairs. The intent of the separation had been to spiritualize the church but not especially to secularize the state.[9]

Once the saints had succeeded in shattering the national church concept, they began to think more and more about claiming for themselves the same authority they had replaced. In 1649 Dell vaguely suggested the fusion of the spheres of grace and nature at some future date after the saints of the Army had become triumphant over the King and Parliament. Drawing from Revelation 11:15, he wrote: "*The* Kingdoms of the World shall become the Kingdoms of the Lord, and of his Christ."[10] Even Collier, who had written in early 1647 that those who make "the Kingdome of Christ to be meerely politicall and a state Kingdome" are wrong, had altered his view by late 1648. Sometime during the preceding twenty-two months he had come to believe that "those who are saved spiritually, know best what is good for the nations temporall well-being, for they seek not their own, but others good."[11]

Saltmarsh did not regard the two spheres of grace and nature as mutually exclusive. As he phrased it, "*grace* destroys not *nature*, yet it *perfects* and *glorifies* nature, and leads it out into higher and more excellent attainments, then it can find in itself."[12] As early as 1644, Saltmarsh had addressed the honorable knights and burgesses for the county of Yorkshire as follows:

> And Such is the quality of your employment, that yee may learn to be at once both Saints, and Statesmen, in this work, for the daily opening of the secrets of affaires before ye, both Religious and civill, may make your House a Senate and a Temple; and the more spiritually ye work in State-affaires, ye act in a higher capacity then common Statesmen, or former Parliaments.[13]

It has been pointed out that the breach between grace and nature was not complete even in the mind of Roger Williams, since he regarded the world of nature as falling within the millenarian scheme.[14] And when Cromwell opened the second Parliament of the Protectorate, he, too, made the point that grace and nature were not mutually exclusive. "If any one whatsoever think the Interest of Christians and the Interest of the Nation inconsistent," he said, "I wish my soul may never enter into his or their secrets!"[15]

The millenarian views of the Army preachers were inarticulate and unsystematic attempts to transmute the theological principle of the reign of Christ into specific political or social terms. This same absence of system can be found at the Putney Debates, where Cromwell professed that he and Ireton were not "wedded and glued to forms of government," a remark borne out by the Lieutenant General's subsequent career. What does appear to be rather definite in millenarian political thought is the criterion of authority for rule. The criterion was the assurance of salvation. Because this assurance of salvation was vouchsafed only to the elect and not to all men, millenarian Antinomianism could be transformed only into political rule by the saintly few.[16]

FUNDAMENTAL LAW AND POWER

Another instance of the inarticulate transmutation of theology into aristocratic polity can be seen in the "power" which the Holy Spirit gave to all of the saints. Historically, the Christian doctrine of grace has carried a twofold meaning: grace as pardon, i.e., forgiveness of sin through God's mercy, and grace as the deification of man through the power of the Holy Spirit.[17] As Erbury put it: "The Son is in them, *God* in their flesh."[18] The term "power" was a favorite with Erbury, Collier, and Dell, especially Dell, who made frequent references to it in nearly all of his sermons. In Dell's theology the receiving of the Spirit was the receiving of the power of God.[19] Francis Cheynell, debating at Oxford with Erbury in 1646, noted that whenever his opponent called the Spirit "the power of God" he was giving expression to the heresy of Socinianism. Cheynell further criticized Erbury for implying that the saints would do greater works through this power of God than even Christ had done because they were adopted heirs of God by Free Grace.[20] The power of the Spirit, said Dell, not only changed man's corrupt nature "as the Fire makes the Iron in which it prevails, like unto it self," but also enabled the believer to do the very same things that Christ did. For Christ said *"all things are possible to him that believeth*; so that a *Believer* hath a kind of *omnipotency*, and all things are possible to him."[21] Certainly Cromwell believed this point of Antinomian theology.

Man of action that Cromwell was, he was also able to state his thoughts upon the power of God:

> I can say this of Naseby, that when I saw the enemy draw up and march in gallant order towards us, and we a company of poor ignorant men, to seek how to order our battle—the General having commanded me to order all the horse—I could not (riding alone about my business) but smile out to God in praises, in assurance of victory, because God would, by things that are not, bring to naught things that are. Of which I had great assurance; and God did it. O that men would therefore praise the Lord, and declare the wonders that He doth for the children of men![22]

The force of these words upon the soldiery of the New Model Army must not be underestimated. The New Model Army was a highly successful fighting machine with a long string of victories from the battle of Naseby to the siege of Oxford, and the soldiers had before them very tangible proof that all things were possible to the power of God. According to Dell the victories of the New Model Army had not been achieved by pikes and muskets but by the Lord's right hand. Erbury asserted that only the "appearance of God in the saints" could yield so many strongholds and conquer so many royal armies in so short a time with so few a number. These were "the proud doers," as Peters called them, whose power was clothed in the sanctity of God.[23]

The anonymous author of a tract entitled *A Little Eye-Salve for the Kingdom* raised the fundamental question of how to distinguish the power of God from other powers in this world.

Instead of leaving the decision to each individual conscience, as Cromwell had done at the Putney Debates when contradictory political ideas were alleged to be the voice of the Spirit, the author supplied a very easy answer. The powers that *be* are ordained of God, he wrote, for they encourage good and discourage evil. But what were men to think when it became apparent that Charles I's power was tyrannous and no longer enjoyed the sustaining power of God? For that contingency, God put His power into the hands of Parliament, which destroyed the King. And when Parliament became just as tyrannical, unjust, and oppressive as the King had been, the solution lay in turn with a third power, the Army:

> I see none of the *power of God* left in the Kingdome, if it be not to be found in the Army: for certainly the *Power of God* did first *set* them up, and since *keep* them up, and made its residence among them, and fought their battailes, and stormed their Cities and strong holds for them: and as *the power of God* hath produced *them* and their *workes,* so *they* againe have acted according to *Gods power.*

To this author the power of God or the seat of sovereignty clearly resided in the Army and not in Parliament.[24]

By early 1649 this was also the position of William Sedgwick. In *A Second View of the Army Remonstrance* Sedgwick affirmed that the Army was not only the whole people of England but also the people of God sanctified by the Holy Spirit. And the power of the people or the Army, he went on, was a superior and stronger power than that of the Parliament which raised up the Army. That such a proposition would seem strange to many, even to the Army itself, Sedgwick freely admitted, but God had made it so. He further conceded in a postscript that this view would seemingly contradict the criticism he had leveled at the Army in his book *The Leaves of the Tree of Life,* written at the time of Saltmarsh's and Pinnell's dramatic departure from its ranks in late 1647. Saltmarsh, it may be recalled, had left the Army after the imprisonment of some of the Levellers at Windsor. This was as close as any chaplain ever came to affiliation with the Levellers. Sedgwick's sympaties were also with the Levellers to some extent, although Sedgwick and Saltmarsh were not so much pro-Leveller as they were opposed to arbitrary action by the Army. Sedgwick felt, for example, that the "*Levellers* are men that are *justly sensible* of the miscarriage of all that are gon before them," but they have "*swarved* and *declined.*" Their truth, Sedgwick continued, was contained in the view that all power and authority ascended out of the people; their falsehood was their enmity to the Lord, expressed through self-love. Only the wisdom of God, of which the Levellers were ignorant, could save the nation.[25]

The most that Sedgwick feared from his remarks on power was apparently the scorn of inconsistency, but Dell was one, it may be recalled, who had been summoned before the House of Lords for preaching, among other things, at Marston that "the power is in you the people; keep it, part not with it." After he was excused from attendance by the Lords, Dell felt constrained to publish his Marston sermon. In his introduction to the printed sermon Dell affirmed that he had put down without abatement the exact substance of the remarks he had delivered at Marston. An examination of it indicates that he did not say what he was charged with saying, that the power was in the people, but rather that the power of the Holy Spirit was in all of the saints. In short, Dell was charged with having imparted a much broader meaning than he originally intended. The same thing happened to him a few months later. In January 1647, when he preached that "every beleever was the Ark of Gods strength," some thought that he had said (or meant) "the Army," instead of "every beleever."[26]

It was probably Hugh Peters who made the most extreme claims regarding the divine source of the power of the Army. On 25 March 1649, Peters, in company with Dr. Robert Massey, a physician, and one Captain Smith of the Army, had occasion to call upon the assistance of Colonel Pride's troops stationed in the Tower of London. While the opportunity was present Peters availed himself of the chance to visit with John Lilburne, a prisoner in the Tower. From the separately published and highly prejudiced accounts of the interlude transcribed by Lilburne and Massey[27] the substance of this interesting meeting can be reconstructed.

After inviting the others to partake of food and drink with his wife and himself, Lilburne remarked that he feared his guest's designs because he knew Peters to be "one of the setting-dogs, or stalking horses of the great men of the Army." Peters protested that he had no design except to advance the glory of God and the good of God's people, the saints. Lilburne complained bitterly to Peters that his imprisonment, in defiance of the Petition of Right, had been accomplished without an accusation, a prosecutor, a witness, or due process of law. In addition it was made all the worse by the humiliation of having sentinels posted at the prison door and by his not being able to see his wife. "And yet, Mr. *Peter,* these are your religious, godly, conscientious Masters," continued Lilburne, "and if this be the fruits of their saint-ship and religion, I do assure you, the Divel is as good, if not a better Saint: for he beleeves and trembles, which is more than I think they do." Peters replied that Lilburne's talk of the Petition of Right meant only that the laws should be nothing but what pleased Lilburne. "Hath not your selfe," said Peters, "exclaimed more then any man against the Lawes, Lawyers, and their Courts in the Kings time, as wicked, cruell, absolute, oppressive and slavish?" Besides, said Peters, observing Lilburne's law books, there *is* no law in England, hastily adding that this was only his private judgment and not the Army's. "No laws!" shouted Lilburne. Wasn't the King's head taken for the very reason that he endeavored to destroy the laws? Yes, this was true, conceded Peters, but some of the laws were, and still are, wicked and slavish.

In the course of the conversation Peters asked Lilburne just what his definition of law was. The Leveller, never at a loss for words, turned to the Parliament's book of *Declarations* and read a passage from a speech by John Pym at the trial of the Earl of Strafford in April 1641:

> The law is that which puts a difference betwixt Good and Evil, betwixt Just and Unjust; if you take away the Law, all things will fall into Confusion, every Man will become a Law to himself, which in the depraved condition of Human Nature, must needs produce many great Enormities; Lust will become a Law, and Envy will become a Law, Covetousness and Ambition will become Laws.[28]

This is no definition of law, said Peters, for it is only a description of its benefits. Then Peters proceeded to give an empirical basis for his own definition of law: "reason deduced and collected from particular events: For necessity you know was, and is the mother of Law." Such a yielding of law to exigency meant to Lilburne that all law could now be equated with the will of Parliament and the Army, i.e., the power of the sword. "There is no Law in this Nation," retorted Peters, "but the sword, and what it gives." The sword must be in someone's hand to enforce the observation of the laws, he continued, and besides, it is honest and good governors who bring the people all the benefits which Pym attributed to the law alone; for if wicked persons are put in places of power, no matter how many or how good the laws are, the people will be unhappy, but if good men are put into high office, even if the laws are defective, there is some presumption that the good men will improve the laws. Lilburne concluded the discussion by announcing his unhesitant choice for good laws rather than good men, just as he had done two years before:

> I had rather live under a very harsh law . . . then live under the moderatest arbitrary government . . . exercised by the godlyest, justest, or choisest men . . . under will and power, by which (by reason of mans corruption, who here hath no perfection, but are subject to actuall backsliding,

and degenerating) I am lyable and in danger every houre
to be distroyed at the pleasure of him that is stronger in
power than I.[29]

Or to put it another way, Lilburne averred his preference for
seven years of rule by the government of Charles I, notwithstanding his execution as a tyrant, rather than live one year under the present government of the Commonwealth.

As early as November 1647, some pro-Royalist newssheets
observed that Peters and Dell had assured a meeting of Army
agitators that they would assist them in an attempt on the King's
life. They had often told the agitators, according to the newssheets, that "Your Majesty is but a dead dogg." These reports
of an alleged plot to make "*a Dead Dog* of a *living Lion*" were
promptly denied by the two chaplains.[30] There seems to be no
evidence that Peters made up his mind that the King should
pay with his life before late October, 1648. A few weeks later,
on 6 December 1648, Colonel Pride and his troops purged the
House of Commons of about 140 of its members, and when some
of the expelled members asked by what authority the Army's
action was taken, Peters replied: "By the power of the Sword."
As Stearns has pointed out, Peters felt, along with John Goodwin, that Pride's Purge was an instance of *Right and Might
Well Met*. The saints were elaborating upon God's design. The
trial of the King was sanctioned by both Peters and Dell, the
latter asserting, according to a petition of the House of Lords
of 20 June 1660, that Christ not Charles was his king. If Venice
and Holland can do without kings, the petition charged Dell
with saying, why not England, too? During a fast and prayer
after the first day of the trial, Peters preached a sermon upon
a text from Psalms 149:5–9:[31]

> 5. Let the saints be joyful in glory: let them sing aloud upon
>   their beds.
> 6. Let the high *praises* of God *be* in their mouth, and a two-
>   edged sword in their hand;

7. To execute vengeance upon the heathen, and punishments upon the people;

8. To bind their kings with chains, and their nobles with fetters of iron;

9. To execute upon them the judgment written; this honour have all his saints. Praise ye the Lord.

On the witness stand Charles Stuart, protesting against the legality of the special court created by Parliament just to try him, claimed that kings cannot be tried by "any Superior Jurisdiction on Earth." The very liberty of the people of England was at stake, said Charles, if they honored the decisions of this illegal court. "For if Power without Law may make Laws, may alter the fundamentall Laws of the Kingdom," Charles stated, "I do not know what subject he is in England, that can be sure of his life or any thing that he calls his owne."[32] On one point, at least, Charles Stuart and John Lilburne stood on common ground.[33]

MIXED GOVERNMENT AND POLICY

That government should be of men (i.e., the saints, and especially the saints of the Army) and not by laws is the central political theme of Peters' published works. In a sermon preached at Islington on 2 August 1646, according to Edwards, Peters said: "*Yee talk of Laws, Laws; the Kingdome is not to be maintained by Lawes, but by perfect men.*"[34] A pamphleteer, commenting on this view a few years later, remarked that good men err every day, and that the best of men are neither infallible nor free from bias.[35] "Some of us may be Planet-struck," wrote Peters, "Yet I hope not principle-shaken."[36] A case in point was the problem of censorship of the press.

In 1647 Peters suggested that some discreet man should be chosen by the Parliament to print the news in the gazettes and courants. He should be assisted by two men from each party—for parties there are, said Peters—in order to avoid scandalous or slanderous affronts. Furthermore, he should be accountable to the state for what he printed or communicated to the kingdom.[37] Apparently, Peters was dissatisfied with the operation of the famous ordinance of 14 June 1643, which prohibited all printing not licensed by the Stationer's Company. Four years later Peters made the same suggestion in his book *Good Work for a Good Magistrate*, provoking Vaughan to remark acidly that had Peters observed his own suggestion, his book would never have seen the press. *"We live now in a* free *Commonwealth,"* said Vaughan, *"where we hope there will be allowed no* such dictators." English law, he continued, has no "Principum placita"—a reference to the medieval constitutional principle *quod principi placet legis habet vigorem,* i.e., what has pleased the prince has the force of law—and wants no "Clericorum placita," whatever Peters may think. One passage in Peters' book specifically denied the charge of dictatorship which Vaughan attributed to it. Peters felt that the affairs of government should be so ordered that one man could be neither above justice nor so powerful that he could not be called to account before a court of justice and properly censured.[38]

Vaughan's "Principum placita" closely resembles the Italian Renaissance political concept of *raison d'état.* In Jacobean England "reason of state" referred to the emergency use of the king's "absolute power," sometimes against the rights of individuals and the common law, in order to promote the common good of the people.[39] In Charles I's reign its connotations were more sinister; it was cited as a ground for imprisoning men by special warrants without due cause shown, for retaining prisoners without bail, and in general for strengthening the royal prerogative. Its opponents, especially Sir Edward Coke after 1621, regarded it as a mask for political dissimulation and treachery, and a device for subordinating means to ends.[40] It was commonly referred to in the language of Elizabethan Machiavellianism as "policy."

The anonymous author of *Anti-Machiavell, or Honesty*

against Policy attested to the Machiavellian "policy" of the New
Model Army "as a mixt body cemented together, with the human morter of interests" and activated by "an Independent intelligence or spirit." The desire of part of the Army to retain its
power was reflected in chaplain Peters, who wrote as early
as 1646 "that the Army was hardly gotten, and I wish it may be
as hardly disbanded." Just a year later he added that nature
commanded the Army's self-preservation, that it could not disband because there was no suitable power to stand between
honest men and their dangers.[41] The reason the Army kept the
power of the sword a little longer was not because of any pe-
cuniary reasons, or "self-ends," wrote the barrister John Cook,
but only because of love for the kingdom. But the Scottish
Presbyterian Robert Baillie felt that the officers and sectaries
followed a "high and bold designe" against disbandment, thanks
to the course of affairs and the light heads of its leaders. "I
blesse God, I know no *Designe* here appearing," wrote Saltmarsh in *A Letter from the Army*, "but *Peace* to the *Kingdome*
. . . The Country cry, *Peace, Peace*, let us have no more Forces
raised to make new Warres." Noting that Sir Gilbert Gerratt
had accused him of hindering the disbandment of General Fairfax's regiment, Saltmarsh added: "I challenge all the *World*
to be able to lay the least of that to my charge."[42]

In *A Vindication of the Army's Remonstrance*, the Army
preacher Collier asked: "Is it not policie as well as piety to take
off those who are enemies to, and obstructers of the peoples
good, the peoples peace?" This was policy in reverse, to be used
by the people for the cause of righteousness rather than by the
King for his own ends. On the other hand, Peters, although accused by Edwards of "Machiavellian tricks," thought it was
wrong to make divinity the handmaiden of policy or the stalking horse for political ends. And Sprigge, speaking in the White-
hall Debates, asserted that whenever men "have measured religion and the appearance of God according to rules and ends of

policy," it has always been the ruin of states.[43] On the whole, references to policy were infrequent among the Army preachers. An exception was Saltmarsh, who as far back as 1639 had written a book, dedicated to Henry Rich, Earl of Holland, entitled *The Practice of Policie in a Christian Life.*

The Practice of Policie is a small collection of political aphorisms which, for example, exhorted men to be sheep in wolves' clothing, to strike while the iron is hot, and, in cases of conspiracy against themselves, to plot divisions among their enemies. He softened these maxims with others to the opposite effect: e.g., dissimulation is not only unlawful but unsafe, be merciful and not revengeful. The true practice of policy, Saltmarsh proclaimed, was an accommodation of one's acts to the model set forth in the Holy Scriptures; such a course would make men capable of philosophy without vanity, oratory without rhetoric, and "Policy" without cunning.[44] A few years later, however, Saltmarsh had less respect for the virtues of policy; he rebuked the eminent divine Thomas Fuller for writing of the reformation of the church "like a *Bodin*, not like *Bucer*; you make it a work of *Policy*, not of *Piety*, of *Reason*, not *Divinity*."[45] In 1646 John Ley told Saltmarsh that his writings violated his own principle of policy set forth in his book. Saltmarsh frankly admitted:

> For some things in my Book of Policy I praise the Lord I can looke on them as on part of the darknesse I was in: And I can freely joyne with any in censuring an unregenerate part in me, as I esteem much of my carnall reason to be. *When I was a childe, I spake as a childe*: neither *have I any fruit* now (as the Apostle sayes) *of some of* these things.[46]

One of the best indices to the strength of the idea of absolute government in the seventeenth century is the strength of its countervailing principle, mixed government, or what later came to be known as the separation of powers. This principle of rule by King, Lords, and Commons made a dramatic appearance in English political life in the reply of Charles I to the Nineteen Propositions. Further statements about it were made by Philip Hunton in his *Treatise of Monarchie* in 1643 and by John Cook in *Redintegratio Amoris* in 1647.[47]

Saltmarsh favored mixed government, although he did not stress the theme, probably because, as he admitted: "I never made State-businesse any Pulpit-work. I never yet preached any thing but Christ."[48] Justice for the kingdom, he wrote, was a "primitive contemperation" of Parliamentary, national, and royal rights; the desired goal was "to keep the mixture even." The late activities of the Anglican divines, by carrying royal rights far beyond "the fundamental and originals in [the] present constitution," had nearly ruined the kingdom.[49] In 1643 Saltmarsh observed with approval the King's suspension from public office, and Parliament's use of its *"fundamentall* power" to carry on the work of the state.[50] This was merely redress for kingly abuse of power. However, in 1646, when Parliament had become predominantly Presbyterian, he wrote that the power of Parliament had exceeded the bounds imposed by its rights and privileges.[51]

Did this mean that private men, who were neither kings nor members of Parliament, were to exercise an increased share in the government? Saltmarsh did not answer this question in 1646, but three years earlier he had written: "I confesse I would not improve their interest too high, nor too soon, for the early settings forth of *private men* is apt to exceed into a tumultuary motion; Yet I would not put them so far behind . . . there are many publick engagements which they are capable on."[52]

For Saltmarsh (as for Sir Edward Coke) the constitution of the English monarchy was of medieval origin, "Breathing to this day, under the succession of so many ages." Therefore, the best way to ensure peace within the state in the future would be to restore this "primitive contemperation" of government which had worked so well in previous centuries.[53] "Reason of state" as a defense of absolute government, either by King or by Parliament, was decomposed by the solvent of mixed government.

Instead of checking man's proclivity toward self-righteousness, most of the Army preachers, and especially Peters, encouraged the saints of the Army to act with the very power and righteousness of God. Within such an institution as a conquering army, in which right and might were conjoined, this concept was particularly fraught with dangerous possibilities for democracy. Lilburne saw the danger clearly, and Saltmarsh was at least aware of the desirability of placing checks and balances on civil rulers. But these individual concepts of government by laws and mixed government stand out in sharp contrast from the predominant belief of those Army preachers who wanted no political trammels on the millenarian rule of the saints.

Masses and Classes

David W. Petegorsky, following R. H. Tawney, has maintained that Puritanism was only the adaptation of religious principles to the needs of economic growth. According to Petegorsky, the rising merchant class found in the Calvinistic division of mankind into elect and non-elect a sanction for the economic class division that was crystallizing between the new middle class and the old feudal order represented by the King and the nobility. The middle class saw itself as materially successful, innately superior, and cleansed by the purifying water of theological doctrine.[1]

Tawney had declared that "the chosen seat of the Puritan spirit seemed to be those classes in society which combined economic independence, education and a certain decent pride in their status."[2] The Antinomian preachers, as purveyors of that branch of Puritanism which stressed the indwelling presence of the Holy Spirit, were more concerned with the poor and oppressed members of society than with the prosperous and educated. They engaged themselves in a three-pronged anti-professional attack upon the educated people: the clergy, the university teachers, and the lawyers. An examination of the Antinomians' interest in social amelioration will help to clarify the basis for these attacks.

Tawney singled out Richard Baxter as an eminent divine whose writings cemented the alliance between God and Mammon. However, as Hudson has shown, Baxter actually counseled his readers to remember that riches were in themselves but dross which leave the wealthy as poor as any man at the grave. The more of your Master's talents you have, wrote Baxter, the more you will finally have to account for; and very few rich men get to heaven.[3] Dell, as we have seen, made much the same point. And Walter Cradock, whose sermons on Antinomianism were very popular in the Army according to Baxter, wrote: "I am afraid some of you make *too much hast to be rich.* . . . oh that you would be exhorted to heare the cause of the poor."[4]

Petegorsky had an explanation for the relation between Antinomianism, or what he termed the chiliastic mysticism of the sectaries, and a concern for the poor and oppressed classes of society. The sectaries, he believed, as the precursors of the true proletarians of the seventeenth century, the Diggers, found it necessary to compensate for their depressed material conditions through a mystical union with God. Because orthodox Calvinism equated the poor with the damned, the sectaries adapted Puritan theology to meet their needs. By substituting an inner spiritual experience for formal education, they extended the possibility of salvation to all men. Once again Calvinism had accommodated itself to the economic conditions of a particular class. The Antinomian chaplains did substitute an inner spiritual experience for formal education as Petegorsky has suggested. They did not, however, proclaim the spiritual equality of all mankind but only the spiritual equality of the saints despite the attacks of their critics that they had interpreted Calvinist theology to mean the salvation of all men.[5]

As early as 2 April 1645 Peters told both Houses of Parliament that the streets were swarming with the poor: why, he asked, should the "Senators of this Citie . . . be so beggarly in the matter of beggars?" On 25 November 1646 William Dell entreated the House of Commons to regard "the oppression of the poor, and the sighing *of the needy.*" England had never seen so much injustice and oppression, he went on; things were so bad that if Parliament would not do God's work in the kingdom, which they had been called to do, God would do it himself without them.[6] Things were indeed bad. During the 1640's poor harvests due to bad weather drove food prices to unprecedented heights while wages rose scarcely at all. Commerce, too, had fallen off badly during the civil war period. "Let us still remember," wrote Peters in his *Last Report*, "the support of Trade is the strength of this Island, discountenance the merchant, and take beggery by the hand."[7]

Generally speaking, however, the chaplains' interest in the poor was peripheral to their other interests. They were not communists in buff-coats of "theological camouflage." In their theology of perfectibility there was no continuous struggle between the forces of good and evil at the barricade of conscience, and certainly no classless millennium. Instead, they fixed their gaze on new revelations of truth which would result in the reign of the saints. Their modification of Calvinism toward the doctrine of the Holy Spirit was designed neither to hasten the overthrow of capitalistic Puritanism nor to compensate, as Petegorsky suggested, for poor environmental conditions. They were primarily trying to guarantee an affirmative answer to the age-old theological question, "Am I saved?"

It is true that Dell and Saltmarsh did share some views, especially the mystical religion of the Spirit, with the famous Digger Gerrard Winstanley. All three men had little use for outward religious forms; all three believed that men could be saved by the power of God alone; both Saltmarsh and Winstanley thought of the millennium in terms of progressive revelations. Nevertheless, neither Dell nor Saltmarsh could have agreed with Winstanley's belief in universal redemption or his economic views. Dell did believe that a "poor mean Christian that earns his bread by hard labour is a thousand times more precious and excellent" than a sinful and unregenerate gentleman, knight, nobleman, or king,[8] but such a statement does not mean that one can equate Antinomianism with any particular social or economic class although it does suggest Dell's own leanings. The disproof of such an equation lies in the devotion to the religion of the Spirit of men like Cromwell, Sir Henry Vane, and Sir Francis Rous, none of them from the dispossessed. At the Putney Debates the concern of Cromwell was not the interest of the poor but the interest of men of property and privilege. "All the main thing that I speak for," said Cromwell's political theorist, Ireton, "is because I would have an eye to property."[9] The Spirit of the Lord recognized no economic barriers.

The interest of the Army preachers in the dispossessed is closely related to their attack upon the clergy, the lawyers, and the university professors. "Clergymen and common Lawyers are the chiefest oppressors," wrote Erbury, "the one by their legall tithes and teachings; the other by their tedious suits and tricks of the Law oppress and plague the Souls and states of Men: besides the Prisoners and the Poor have heavy oppressors, and are Chief among the oppressed."[10] David Ogg has stated that the Puritans were socially little better than pariahs, and that their main motive (except for the lawyers) in establishing the New Jerusalem was antiprofessionalism.[11] The eminent Presbyterian Robert Baillie was convinced from long experience that the spirit which guided sectaries such as Dell into church reformation would press them on to pull down the state as well: "*Wee need not speak of their declared rage against Universities and all Societies of Learning, against the Society of Merchant-adventurers, against the Common-Councell and Court of Alder-men in the City of London: all these things to them are corrup-tions, and grievances to be extirpate.*"[12]

Petegorsky has suggested that after the substitution of the Scriptures, which could be read by the literate and educated, for the formal education of church prelates as the final author-ity in religious life, the illiterate and uneducated poor had no path to the truth save by the power of the Holy Spirit. This thesis may have some validity in the New Model Army. It seems likely that a majority of the soldiers in the infantry regiments of the New Model could not even write their names; but the members of the cavalry regiments, who took the lead in the

political movements in 1647 and after, had many men of some
education among them.[13] Some evidence of the antipathy between Antinomianism and academic learning in the Army can
be noted in the presence of the numerous "mechanick" or lay
preachers, such as Paul Hobson the cobbler, who, as artisans,
preached the gospel of Free Grace.[14] One of the best examples
of Petegorsky's view of spiritual religion and education can be
found in Dell.

The university now as in the days of Wycliffe, Hus, and
Luther, wrote Dell, has the same heathenish and anti-Christian
doctrine ruled over by Aristotle.[15] The study of Aristotle (who
is dead and damned yet remains exalted by the authority of
Thomas Aquinas) emphasized free will and natural philosophy
rather than Christ. John Webster, who may have been a chaplain in the Army, also attacked Aristotle's influence in the universities, on the ground that an understanding of the mysteries
of the kingdom of heaven could only be achieved through the
Holy Spirit. "To this I know it will be objected," wrote Webster, "That *Schools* teach the knowledge of tongues, without
which the Scriptures (being originally written in the *Hebrew*
and *Greek*) cannot be truly and rightly translated, expounded,
nor interpreted: and therefore it is necessary that *Schools* and
Academies should teach these, as properly and mainly con-
ducible to this end." However, Webster felt that languages had
been changed and altered as "fashions and garments." Besides,
he added, whoever relies upon a translator is the same as one
who relies upon a teacher.[16]

Liberal education, wrote Dell, with its study of language
and the sciences, with its degrees and ordinations, does not
change one iota the corrupt and evil nature in which its minions
and practitioners were born; learning alone, without the power
of the Holy Spirit, was insufficient preparation for the ministry.
Saltmarsh, too, while admonishing men not to despise one another for learning, conceded that he allowed learning its place
anywhere in the kingdom of the world, but not in the kingdom

of God.[17] Even John Lilburne believed that the truth of the gospel of Christ was "too homely a thing" for the great and learned doctors of the world to embrace.[18] Winstanley called the universities "standing ponds of stinking waters."[19] Chaplain Erbury's followers were so hostile to formal learning that the debate between Erbury and Cheynell at Oxford had to be moved from the "publick Schools" to a church (albeit the University church) before they would attend it.[20]

If all divinity is swaddled in human learning, or if learning is an art to deceive and abuse the understanding of men, as the Leveller Walwyn believed, then how shall poor plain people, who have not the leisure (or, it might be added, money) to attain a formal education, be saved? "Ignorance," answered Dell, "*is more fit and ready to receive the Gospel, than Wisdom.*"[21] Nevertheless, Dell's attack upon learning as a prerequisite for the ministry did not mean that he, or indeed Webster, was against secular learning. They simply made a sharp separation between religious and secular knowledge, just as Dell and Saltmarsh had done between the spheres of grace and nature in the toleration controversy. For instance, Dell advocated a college or university for every large English city: London, York, Bristol, Exeter, and Norwich. In these colleges and universities, which should receive a "competent maintenance" from the state, the liberal arts and sciences would be taught to twenty persons instead of one in order to make men serviceable to the commonwealth. These colleges were not to be erected for the purpose of achieving salvation or training men for the ministry. Furthermore, they would be taught by "Godly and Learned Men."[22] There is no doubt but that Dell included himself within this group of "Godly and Learned Men" after he became the Master of Gonville and Caius College, Cambridge, in 1649. (On his qualifications for the post Baxter observed that "*Reason, Sound Doctrine, Order, and Concord*" were the greatest strangers to Dell's mind.[23] The utilitarian role in education can also be found in Webster's thought. The subject which had the greatest practical value for him was natural philosophy or natural science; his mentor was Francis Bacon. Peters, too, respected Bacon and was for the extension of learning, but the academies he proposed, unlike Dell's, were to teach piety and righteousness, and were to be for the nobility and gentry.[24]

The Antinomian attack upon the universites ran strictly counter to the traditional Puritan emphasis upon a "Godly and Learned" ministry. It has been suggested that during the period 1640–60 the Puritans *in the main* were not arrayed against an educated ministry or critical of the universities.[25] Nevertheless, thc New Model chaplains, the Levellers, and the Diggers did attack them. What is more ironical, most of the chaplains who condemned university education were themselves educated in universities. Peters even helped to found Harvard College.

A second major aspect of the anti-professionalism upon which the chaplains, especially Peters, and the Levellers and the Diggers found themselves in agreement was the subject of reform and administration of the law. In 1646 an anonymous pamphleteer observed that after five years of contact between the King and Parliament the commonalty were still enslaved by the arbitrary will and power of a few mercenary lawyers. These lawyers charged the iniquitous fee of ten or twenty shillings irrespective of whether or not their services were worth it. "It is therefore to be considered," continued the author, "whether it be agreeable to justice, and the freedom and prosperity of this Nation, that the prosperity and flourishing state of a few Lawyers, Atturneys, Jaylours, and their adherents should be preserved before, the just liberty, peace, and well being of this whole Nation and their posterities."[26] Collier complained in 1647 "that to seek a Remedy" in the courts of law "proves worse than the disease; many an honest man chusing rather to suffer losse." Ogg has suggested that the lawyer's profits came largely from conveyancing—the practice of examining titles of property, giving opinions about their validity, and drawing deeds for their transfer. The remedy seemed to be a Land Registry which would obviate inquiries into the title of property.[27] The cure of the Buckinghamshire Levellers and Peters for this situation was set forth in Peters' pamphlet *A Word for the Armie*. Peters wanted to keep local records in all counties of all men's estates and alienations, which should in turn be transmitted to "a grand or leiger Record at Westminster." This would avoid the delay and expense of taking cases to the quarterly courts at Westminster.[28]

It was not only the lawyers but the law itself that drew fire from the critics. The severity of the criminal code then, as in Bentham's day, was a cause of serious complaint. It was Peters' view, as well as that of the Leveller Overton,[29] that prisoners for debt should be "dispatched" and not lose their heads or their hands. Poor thieves should not be hanged but usefully employed or banished. A second grievance, implicit in the anti-Normanism of the Levellers, was the language of the law—a continuous reminder of its Norman origin. It is a real oppression, wrote Collier, that the French should be better read in English laws than Englishmen are.[30] Finally, much agitation arose over the evils of the Court of Chancery for the delays in justice which came about as a result of labyrinthine procedure. One Leveller's advice was to make the laws "certain, short, and plain," and Peters wrote: "Quicke Justice makes quiet Commonwealths, for this keeps Hollanders happy under heavy taxes."[31]

Peters' attitude toward legal reform in 1646 underwent something of a change in the next few years. Massey reported that Peters, while visiting Lilburne in the Tower of London, told "Free-born John" that they had fought against the King in order to be free from the laws, which were tyrannous, and not for the continuation or preservation of them.[32] Two years later Peters went so far as to advocate the burning of all the old records in the Tower as monuments of tyranny and sin. (Unfortunately, his suggestions on legal reform have been remembered largely for this malapert advice.) One of the sparks from

Peters' pen on the subject of law reform in 1651 ignited the imagination of Winstanley. The immediate provocation for Winstanley's utopian work *The Law of Freedom*, as its author freely acknowledged, was the suggestion of Peters that law and government should be adapted to the Holy Scriptures.[33] On 20 January 1651 a Commonwealth law reform committee, including Sir Matthew Hale, Anthony Ashley Cooper, and Peters, was appointed. Bulstrode Whitelock, who often advised this committee, recorded in his *Memorials* that Peters was very active on the committee, was highly opinionated, and understood very little of the law. He would frequently mention some Dutch legal proceedings about which he was completely mistaken.[34]

The third major manifestation of anti-professionalism by the chaplains, the Levellers, and the Diggers was directed against the tithing clergy. Winstanley, for example, believed that the payment of tithes was "the greatest sin of oppression."[35] The significance of the opposition to the tithe, and the opposition often included in 1647 some of the ejected ministry, lay in the opposition to church organization, for the tithe was the tenth part of the annual produce paid as a tax for the support of the clergy and religious institutions. Those who supported tithes, and they often included ministers put into confiscated livings, feared that tenants who asked to be relieved of paying tithes would soon ask to be relieved of paying rent. In the summer of 1647 Parliament, in response to the complaints from several counties by ministers unable to collect tithes, passed an act giving Justices of the Peace power to enforce tithes for ministers put into sequestered livings. After the passage of this act petitions, bearing clear traces of Leveller influence, marked the anti-tithe agitation. Indeed, both the second and third Agreements of the People as well as the Heads of Proposals proposed the abolition of tithes.[36] Collier argued that the collection of tithes for the "belly-gods" was against both the law and the gospel, against conscience, and furthermore, "the people groan under it as an oppression." Saltmarsh indicated his opposition by relinquishing his claim against the state for a year's arrearage of tithes. Erbury wrote a book some years later entitled *The Grand Oppressor, or, the Terror of Tithes*. Peters and Dell, according to the newssheet *Mercurius Elencticus*, were against tithes, yet Dell took £200 per annum from his living at Yelden.[37]

The Antinomian chaplains were in close agreement with the Levellers in their concern for the poor and their antiprofessionalism. But where the Levellers were concerned with the political and economic reconstruction of society, the chaplains were primarily absorbed in the continuous search for further assurances of salvation. Their antiprofessionalism, and their interest in the poor, stemmed primarily from their theology, which stressed the direct manifestation of the Holy Spirit in the human conscience rather than a reliance upon professional groups. "For God doth not consider men as the World doth, to wit, as they are *Tradesmen*, or *Gentlemen*, or *Scholars*, or *Clergymen*," wrote Dell, "but he considers men as Believers, or Unbelievers."[38]

Conclusion

Of the nine pairs of politico-religious polarities by which we undertook to measure the degree to which the chaplains were authoritarian or democratic, the authoritarian tradition prevailed in six: authority took precedence over liberty, power over law, millenarianism over separatism, sainthood over equality, grace over covenant, and anarchy over elective polity. In only three instances was the democratic tradition predominant: unity took precedence over uniformity, the masses over the classes, and mixed government over policy.

There were, as Richard Baxter suspected, some affinities between the Army chaplains and Leveller democracy, especially on the subject of religious toleration. Against the policies of a Parliament which (if hesitant about Presbyterians) was consistently Erastian in outlook, both Dell and Saltmarsh separated the spheres of grace and nature—man's relation to God and man's relation to man. The Antinomian preachers agreed upon a fundamental unity of theological belief, which they felt would bridge eventually all essential points of difference, rather than a uniformity of ecclesiastical forms, which they felt resulted in persecution by the civil magistrate. All truth, thought the chaplains, had not yet been disclosed to man and would not be until the second coming of Christ, which seemed imminent. Nevertheless, while waiting for new revelations of theological truth, the Antinomians turned the antennae of their consciences to fresh but fragmentary manifestations of truth as revealed by the Holy Spirit. And should disagreements arise, the chaplains urged free debates and discussion as well as a free press (though not by majority votes and not by "common *consent* or voyce") so that forbearance could not give way to coercion. But even Saltmarsh's concept of truth, which could be derived from free debate and discussion, was circumscribed by certain boundaries which robbed it of a great deal of its force for modern democracy. For example, he was not prepared to tolerate or entertain *all* views, especially those of the papists or heathen. However, in such a debate or discussion Saltmarsh's conscience was an oracle no less fit for the Spirit of the Lord than Cromwell's. And the Army preacher told the Lieutenant-General as much even on a political issue, the imprisonment of the Levellers after the Ware mutiny. Such individualism as this contributed to the Leveller spirit if not to Leveller doctrine.

Besides individualism, there was also a spiritual equality in Antinomian thought which, at least in theory, looked upon all of the saints alike irrespective of their economic or social status. The only important thing was that the Holy Spirit was operative in a man's heart. But the chaplains themselves were not quite so impartial. They set forth numerous social reforms of the law, tithing, and education in behalf of the poor and downtrodden. And although their attack upon the professional classes (lawyers, clergymen, and university professors) stemmed in part from a religious anti-intellectualism, it was not necessarily anti-intellectual in the secular sense; some of them specifically favored secular education—in one instance along scientific lines. At Putney it was very hard to tell the difference between the Spirit of God and human reason. The chaplains were inclined to turn their backs on reason, to root it out, to have it clearly distinguished from God's Spirit. Therefore, whenever an impasse was reached at Putney, the solution oftentimes would be to call a prayer meeting in order to seek new revelations of divine truth. The Army preachers, then, despite their sympathy for the poor, recognized no economic or social background as having a prior claim to or being a sign of God's favor. Cromwell, from the gentry, and Hobson, a cobbler, were equally moved by the Lord's Spirit.

Despite all this, there is some fairly strong evidence that the Army preachers were not exponents of what Baxter called "State Democracy." It is difficult to see how deterministic Antinomian theology—providing for no good works and no free will—could profess to allow any place for a belief in political liberty even though the abrogation of the law of Moses resulted in Christian liberty with God. And, furthermore, in reducing to a cipher man's role in the salvation process, the Antinomians did not seem inclined to point up the political responsibilities of men in the state. To be sure, Dell stated that this spiritual impotence did not make man any "the less" in the kingdoms of this world; but the others, and very likely Dell himself, did not believe that defiance of the civil magistrate could be justified in the name of the Holy Spirit. Nor did the chaplains believe in a *jus divinum*—a supreme overriding law, a fundamental law carrying certain natural rights—which would impose restrictions upon a civil magistrate. This was true even though, ironically, as members of the Army they were involved in open rebellion against the English sovereign. The power of God clearly seemed to reside in the Army, and ultimately, Peters and Dell, as members of it, sanctioned the execution of the King.

Antinomian theology, with its hope through revelation for the complete removal of the stigma of original sin, resulted in a belief in the perfectibility of the saints. And although this was not extended to all men—indeed only to a few—it was the basis for a very optimistic outlook about the nature of those few. By minimizing the sinfulness in human nature, the chaplains escaped the paralyzing effect that a belief in total depravity gives to the saints' capacity for intelligent thought and action, but it was not a view of human nature which recognized their limitations, especially in statecraft. Only John Saltmarsh had any conception of the possible abuses of saintly power which ultimately might come with Army rule. By opposing the concept of policy or *raison d'état*, which he had once supported, with a sympathetic attitude toward the notion of mixed government, Saltmarsh significantly recognized the dangers inherent in the position the other chaplains took, namely, identifying the power of God with the power of the Army. The others, as their opponents charged, tended to adopt an easy optimism about the goodness of the saints without feeling the need for limitations upon authority.

Despite the separation of nature and grace in the thought of Dell and Saltmarsh, which it appears had been largely formulated to counteract theocratic Presbyterianism, nearly all of the Antinomian preachers wrote of some kind of millenarian kingdom of the saints. Once the Army became dominant over the King and Parliament, Dell's grace-nature dichotomy dissolved into a nebulous polity of government by the saints. It was Hugh Peters who made the most articulate elaboration upon the millenarian designs of the saints in political government; he believed in government by good men rather than good laws. While Dell and Collier saw the fusion of nature and grace leading to the rule of the children of light, Saltmarsh firmly resisted any temptation to make the spiritual kingdom of Christ into a temporal government of saints. Because faith was an effect, not a cause, of God's saving grace in Antinomian theology, the Army saints possessed in theory a greater certitude of salvation than the followers of Federal Covenant theology. This certitude almost led to the identification of the saints so that they could be singled out, conceivably, for special political rule over the rest of society. Although all of the chaplains were not prepared to go this far, nevertheless in the 1650's the Fifth Monarchy men, who drew heavily from the Antinomian tradition, did state this goal in more specific political terms.

Nor has the use of the analogical method been found to be effective in demonstrating the relationship of Puritanism and democracy. First of all, the rejection of Covenant theology by the Army chaplains made impossible an analogy with a social contract between the ruler and the governed. The chaplains did not frame their thoughts in contractual terms—not even Hugh Peters, who in New England had been a subscriber to

Covenant theology. Second, it is extremely difficult to talk about political equality emerging from a religious concept that recognized both saints and sinners, even when some erroneously believed that Arminianism made it possible for all sinners to become saints. Third, the use of analogy in connection with polity also has its problems. For one thing, Saltmarsh seriously doubted if "in *spirituals,* as in Civils, Votes and Voyces are to make Laws." Although the use of analogy may lead, in the case of Independent congregations, to the popular election and removal of civil magistrates, it may in the Presbyterian church lead to the management of the church by those in authority and not the people. Also, assuming the principle of analogy to work with reference to the ecclesiastical polity of the chaplains, it would lead logically not to democracy but to anarchy, for the chaplains were not interested in any specific church form. And finally, those chaplains who were prepared to oppose the place of learning or formal education in the salvation process, or, as in Dell's case, stated that ignorance was more fit to receive the gospel than wisdom, were hardly the people who could be said, by the process of analogy, to be making a pronounced contribution to the intellectual life of the secular sphere.

Antinomianism, then, failed to transmute its theology into concrete political terms. Its failure was also Cromwell's failure during the Commonwealth and Protectorate. Cromwell had admitted at the Putney Debates that he was not "wedded and glued to forms of [civil] government." His subsequent career was a testimony to that pragmatic view. Cromwell never concealed his hostility to the egalitarian legalism of the Levellers, and he increasingly emphasized, as did Antinomian theology, this criterion of authority for rule—the saint's assurance of salvation. The apotheosis of this idea was, of course, the famous Nominated or Barebones Parliament of Saints. Its downfall within six months arose from differences between the Parliamentary saints and Cromwell over the aforementioned social reforms, just as the *Agreement of the People* had failed at

Putney because of differences between Cromwell and the Levellers over political reforms. The voice of God was not always clear.

Although Cromwell did not find a satisfactory and permanent political form of rule after he assumed the responsibilities of government, he did fare considerably better with his Antinomian principles in the realm of religious liberty. Many of the sects of the Commonwealth and Protectorate, such as the Diggers, Ranters, Fifth Monarchists, and Quakers, drew heavily upon the mystical and millennial outlook of Antinomianism, but some of the members of these sects, who carried their enthusiasm to extremes, represented threats to public order and morality. There was the communitarian economic experiment of Gerrard Winstanley, the ranting offence against Christian sexual morality of Lawrence Clarkson, the subversive political tendency of John Rogers, and the prophetic role of the Quaker James Naylor. In the face of such extremism, Cromwell manifested sympathy with and an accessibility to many of these sectarians.

In the religious realm, Antinomianism gave Cromwell insights which enabled him to establish among the sects an enviable record for religious toleration for that day. The Antinomian heritage for political affairs tended to be anarchical, and while this might provide a fighting faith for a righteous Army to overthrow the existing order, it was far less effective as a basis for promoting political stability. The dilemma which Cromwell faced, but only partially resolved, was best expressed by his Army chaplain, Saltmarsh, in his *Dawnings of Light* (p. 36): "The Government of Christ seems to be framed as neither tyranny should get in at any *consociation,* nor *anarchy,* or *libertinisme* get in at any *dissociation,* or particular gathering, and at this beam we may weigh our controversies of this age."

Notes

INTRODUCTION

1. Notably, G. P. Gooch, *English Democratic Ideas in the Seventeenth Century*, 2d ed. (1927); Rufus M. Jones, *Mysticism and Democracy in the English Commonwealth* (1932); A. D. Lindsay, *The Modern Democratic State* (1943); James H. Nichols, *Democracy and the Churches* (1951); Ralph B. Perry, *Puritanism and Democracy* (1944); David W. Petegorsky, *Left-Wing Democracy in the English Civil War* (1940); D. B. Robertson, *The Religious Foundations of Leveller Democracy* (1951); A. S. P. Woodhouse, *Puritanism and Liberty*, 2d ed. (1951).

2. Richard B. Schlatter, ed., *Richard Baxter and Puritan Politics* (1957); Norman Cohn, *The Pursuit of the Millennium* (1957); Leo F. Solt, "Puritanism and Democracy in the New Model Army," in a forthcoming issue of *Archiv für Reformationgeschichte*.

3. For example, Winthrop S. Hudson, "Theological Convictions and Democratic Government," *Theology Today*, X (1953), 230-39; Nichols, *Democracy and the Churches*, pp. 270-71; Woodhouse, *Puritanism and Liberty*, Introduction; Reinhold Niebuhr, *Christian Realism and Political Problems*, p. 101; Joseph Frank, *The Levellers*, pp. 248-49.

CHAPTER ONE

1. *Reliquiae Baxterianae*, pp. 50, 53. Full titles and publication data will be found in the Bibliography, pp. 123-41.

2. Woodhouse, *Puritanism and Liberty*, Introduction, p. 18.

3. *Camden Miscellany*, Vol. VIII, quoted in Charles H. Firth, *Cromwell's Army*, 2d ed., p. 317.

4. Edward Hyde, Earl of Clarendon, *The History of the Rebellion and Civil Wars in England*, IV, 237.

5. George Yule, *The Independents in the English Civil War*, pp. 11–19.

6. Leonard J. Trinterud, "The Origins of Puritanism," *Church History*, XX (1951), 52.

7. Baxter, *Reliquiae*, pp. 51, 53. For a list of the battles at which Baxter was present, see Frederick J. Powicke, *A Life of the Reverend Richard Baxter*, I, 73–78.

8. Baxter, *Reliquiae*, pp. 56, 57, 53, 59; Thomas Edwards, *Gangraena*, Part III, p. 45.

9. The correct name was not Peters, but Peter. However, Peter's contemporaries and Peter himself frequently spelled it "Peters," which is the spelling I have adopted. See Raymond P. Stearns, *The Strenuous Puritan*, p. 10.

10. Raymond P. Stearns, ed., "Letters and Documents by or Relating to Hugh Peter," *The Essex Institute Historical Collections*, LXXII (1936), 59; Godfrey Davies, "The Army of the Eastern Association, 1644–5," *English Historical Review*, XLVI (1931), 90.

11. Stearns, *The Essex Institute Historical Collections*, LXXII, 59. Dell, *The Building, Beauty, Teaching and Establishment of the Truly Christian and Spiritual Church*, p. 74.

12. John and John Archibald Venn, *Alumni Cantabrigienses*, Part I, IV, 10.

13. See H. John McLachlan, *Socinianism in Seventeenth-Century England*, pp. 226–33. Erbury was born in Glamorganshire and studied at Brasenose College, Oxford. Later he was vicar of St. Mary's in Cardiff, and Walter Cradock, a friend of Richard Baxter, was his curate. In 1634 Archbishop Laud reported to the King in his *Annual Accounts of His Province* that Erbury had been admonished by the bishop of Llandaff for his and his curate's schismatical preaching. Four years later he was forced to resign his living. Christopher Love, in return for past favors, befriended Erbury after he was "plundered" in Wales and procured for him a chaplaincy in Major-General Skippon's regiment at the usual chaplain's pay of eight shillings a day. Edwards recorded that Erbury broached many Antinomian doctrines while in the Earl of Essex's Army (*Gangraena*, Part I, p. 77). Erbury left the Army and lived in London in 1645, but at least by the surrender of Oxford he had returned to the Army once more.

14. Anthony à Wood (*Athenae Oxonienses*, II, 761) said Sprigge was a retainer to Fairfax, but Clement Walker (*The Compleat History of Independency*, p. 32) called Sprigge the chaplain to Fairfax. Webster is discussed in Jones, *Mysticism and Democracy*, pp. 85–90; probably on the authority of the *DNB*, *s.v.*, Jones states that Webster was a chaplain for a period in the Parliamentary Army. Edwards (*Gangraena*, Part III, p. 242) listed both Symonds and Cradock as chaplains. Cradock's sermon in Wales on 7 July 1645 attempted to enlist His Majesty's soldiers to take up arms in defense of Parliament (*The True Informer* [5–12 July 1645], p. 93).

15. Collier's sermon preached at the Army headquarters at Putney on 29 September 1647 was later printed as *A Discovery of the New Creation*. All the evidence seems to indicate that Denne was a cornet rather than a chaplain (see, for example, *Mercurius Pragmaticus*, 22–29 May 1649). Powell preached to the Parliamentary forces on the island of Anglesey in 1647. For an excellent monograph on Walter Cradock and Vavasor Powell, see Geoffrey Nuttall, *The Welsh Saints, 1640–1660*.

16. *History of the Rebellion*, IV, 237.

17. *A Brief Discovery*, pp. 10, 19, 21.

18. *Mercurius Elencticus*, 6–13 February 1649, quoted in William Y. Tyndall, *John Bunyan, Mechanik Preacher*, p. 74.

19. *The Cleere Sense* (1645).

20. Sprigge, *Anglia Rediviva*, p. 180.

21. *Memorials of the English Affairs*, new ed., I, 579; *Mr. Peters Message*, p. 1; *Two Letters Sent to the Honoble William Lenthal, Esq.*, p. 7.

22. Edwards, *Gangraena*, Part I, p. 98; [William Prynne], *A Brief Justification of the XI. Accused Members*, p. 8; *Works of Darkness Brought to Light*, p. 8; [William Prynne], *VIII Queries*, p. 6; [William Prynne], *Minors No Senators*, p. 16.

23. *A Key to the Cabinet of the Parliament*, p. 2.

24. *Master Peters Messuage from Sir Thomas Fairfax*, p. 1.

25. Sprigge, *Anglia Rediviva*, p. 102. The most recent and most comprehensive biography of Hugh Peters is the excellent work of Raymond P. Stearns, *The Strenuous Puritan*. Peters was born in 1598 at Fowey, Cornwall. At fifteen he entered Trinity College, Cambridge, and in 1622 he received the M.A. degree. Called to task by Bishop Montaigne for his criticism of the religious practices of the new Catholic queen, Henrietta Maria, Peters reaffirmed his Anglican convictions. Before leaving England for Holland in order to join other non-Separatist Congregational ministers in exile, Peters worked in support of a plan to raise money to buy impropriations in order to give the Puritan faction greater power within the Church. In the winter of 1627–28 Peters associated himself with the English church classis in Holland, which was largely modeled after the Congregational type of church organization. Although Peters' church at Rotterdam was remarkably free from commitments to either Anglican or Reformed church theological beliefs, it aroused Archbishop Laud's wrath, and the classis soon fell apart. By 1635 Peters was on his way to New England, and in December 1636, he took the post of minister at Salem, which had been vacated by Roger Williams. Three years later Peters issued a list of excommunicates from the Salem congregation. Among these was Williams, who had long since fled the colony. During the Antinomian controversy in 1636, Peters testified that Mrs. Anne Hutchinson had accused him and other ministers of preaching a "covenant of works" whereas John Cotton preached a "covenant of grace" (Charles Francis Adams, ed., *Antinomianism in the Colony of Massachuestts Bay*, p. 246; Perry Miller, *The New England Mind from Colony to Province*, p. 59).

26. John Vicars, *The Burning-Bush Not Consumed*, p. 357; *Mr. Peters Message*, p. 11; Whitelock, *Memorials*, I, 562; *Mr. Peters Report from Bristol*, p. 3.

27. *A Perfect Diurnall of Some Passages in Parliament* (16–23 March 1646), p. 1110; *Commons' Journals*, IV, 583–84.

28. Sedgwick was born in Bedfordshire and was educated at Pembroke

College, Oxford. In about 1634 he became rector of Farnham in Essex, but in 1642 he was enrolled as chaplain to Sir William Constable's regiment in the Earl of Manchester's Army. On 17 January 1645, Cromwell, as the Governor of Ely, wrote to the sequestrators of the Isle of Ely, entreating them to pay two chaplains, one of whom was Sedgwick, the money which the Earl of Manchester had given them a warrant to receive. Sedgwick may have become the chaplain to Cromwell's own regiment when Baxter refused that position.

29. *Perfect Occurrences of Both Houses of Parliament and Martiall Affairs,* 22–29 May 1646, 5–12 June 1646.

30. [Dell], *A Vindication,* pp. 3–4, 6–7; Dell, *Building, Beauty,* p. 68.

31. *The Writings and Speeches of Oliver Cromwell,* I, 404. Dell had received his M.A. degree and had become a Fellow at Emmanuel College, Cambridge, in 1631. Little is known of his activities until he joined the New Model Army. Before his Army service he had been serving as minister at Yelden in Bedfordshire.

32. *Lords' Journals,* VIII, 401, 403, 418; [Dell], *A Vindication,* pp. 8, 13.

33. Edwards, *Gangraena,* Part III, p. 262; Prynne, *The Sword of Christian Magistracy Supported,* "Epistle Dedicatory."

34. *Lords' Journals,* VIII, 422, 432, 433, 436.

35. Speech IV, Carlyle, II, 417, quoted in Godfrey Davies, *The Early Stuarts,* p. 125.

36. See *Mr. Peters Message,* p. 5; Saltmarsh, *A Letter from the Army,* p. 4; Dell, *Building, Beauty,* pp. 72–74; Erbury, *The Lord of Hosts,* p. 14.

37. Robert Barclay, *Inner Life of the Religious Societies of the Commonwealth,* p. 165.

38. Ram, *The Soldier's Catechism,* pp. 21–22, quoted in Firth, *Cromwell's Army,* p. 330.

39. *Calendar of State Papers* (Venetian), XXVII, 190.

40. Peters, *A Word for the Armie,* p. 10; Firth, *Cromwell's Army,* p. 37.

41. Samuel R. Gardiner, *History of the Great Civil War,* III, 38, 43.

42. [Oliver Cromwell and Hugh Peters], *A Coppie of Lieut. Gen. Cromwels Letter: Concerning the Taking of Winchester Castle,* p. 6.

43. See Gardiner, *History of the Great Civil War,* III, 42.

44. George Johnson ("From Seeker to Finder," unpublished Ph.D. thesis, University of Chicago, 1948, p. 24) lists several soldiers of the Army who wrote tracts similar in religious content to the writings of Saltmarsh and Dell.

45. Firth, *Cromwell's Army,* p. 7.

46. William Haller and Godfrey Davies, eds., *The Leveller Tracts, 1647–1653,* pp. 55, 63, 57.

47. *The Kingdomes Weekly Intelligencer* (3–10 August 1647), p. 23.

48. Maurice Ashley, *John Wildman, Plotter and Postmaster,* p. 19.

49. Haller and Davies, *Leveller Tracts*, p. 78.
50. Woodhouse, *Puritanism and Liberty*, pp. 54, 53, 69.
51. *Ibid.*, pp. 438, 73; [Saltmarsh], *Englands Friend Raised from the Grave.*
52. See Haller and Davies, *Leveller Tracts*, p. 178.
53. [Saltmarsh], *Wonderfull Predictions*, pp. 1–5; Fuller, *The Worthies of England* (ed. John Freeman), p. 665; Stearns, *The Essex Institute Historical Collections*, LXXII, 133 n.; Wood, *Athenae*, II, 289.
54. A native of Yorkshire, Saltmarsh was educated at Magdalene College, Cambridge, where he received the M.A. degree. Philip Nye, later one of the "dissenting brethren" of the Westminster Assembly, had been his teacher. In about 1639 Saltmarsh became rector of Heslerton in Yorkshire. In 1636 he published a volume of academic verse, and in 1643 a poem entitled "A Divine Rapture," welcoming the Solemn League and Covenant; Wood called him "no contemptible poet" (*Athenae*, II, 287). After resigning his Yorkshire preferment because of scruples about taking tithes, Saltmarsh preached in and around Northampton. By January 1645, he was located in the rectory of Brasted, Kent.
55. Lilburne, *The Peoples Prerogative and Priviledges*, p. 58; *Mercurius Pragmaticus* ([16–23 November 1647], p. 72) listed Saltmarsh, Dell, Lilburne, Overton, and others as "Levelling agitating brethren."
56. *Mr. William Sedgwicks Letter to His Excellency Thomas Lord Fairfax.*
57. Charles H. Firth, ed., *Clarke Papers*, XLIX, 3.
58. Wood, *Athenae*, II, 464.
59. Pp. 42, 44. Collier expressed sentiments very similar to those of Saltmarsh and Sedgwick; see his *General Epistle*, pp. 81–82.
60. *The Peoples Prerogative*, p. 58.
61. Pinnell, *A Word of Prophesy*, pp. 4, 5, 8.
62. Jubbes, *An Apology*, p. 2.
63. *Mercurius Elencticus* (12–19 January 1648). The twelve ministers were William Carter, Richard Symonds, John Goodwin, Thomas Goodwin, Sydrach Simpson, Samuel Bolton, Stephen Marshall, Philip Nye, a Mr. Strong, a Mr. Whitaker, a Mr. Salloway, and a Mr. Carroll. Thomas Goodwin, Nye, and Simpson were members of the "dissenting brethren" of the Westminster Assembly. Symonds was an Antinomian who knew Walter Cradock, and John Goodwin was regarded as an Arminian.
64. Dell, *Building, Beauty*, p. 74.
65. John Bastwick, *The Utter Routing of the Whole Army*, "The Antiloquie."

CHAPTER TWO

1. See *The City of God*, Everyman ed., II, 153–54.
2. Arthur Barker, *Milton and the Puritan Dilemma*, p. 323.

3. Everett H. Emerson, "Calvin and Covenant Theology," *Church History*, XXV (1956), 141. However, Emerson adds that many of the implications of Covenant theology are present in Calvin's work.

4. Trinterud, *Church History*, XX, 50, 45. John D. Eusden (*Puritans, Lawyers, and Politics*, pp. 30–31) suggests that Covenant theology did not flourish until after 1630.

5. The classic treatment of Federal theology is Perry Miller, *The New England Mind, the Seventeenth Century*, especially chap. xiii.

6. Stephen Geree, *The Doctrine of the Antinomians*, p. 6.

7. *The Honey-Combe of Free Justification by Christ Alone*, p. 25.

8. *The Letters and Journals of Robert Baillie*, II, 117; Baxter, *Reliquiae*, p. 111.

9. Dell, *The Crucified and Quickned Christian*, p. 317; Saltmarsh, *An End of One Controversie*, p. 116.

10. Jerald C. Brauer, "Puritan Mysticism and the Development of Liberalism," *Church History*, XIX (1950), 153.

11. George A. Johnson, "From Seeker to Finder," *Church History*, XVII (1948), 300–301.

12. *Reliquiae*, p. 111.

13. William Haller, "The Word of God in the New Model Army," *Church History*, XIX (1950), 28.

14. "Now Christ thus loving the soul . . . is called *Free Grace* indeed; when the Father shall freely give his Son, and the Son freely his Heart-blood, and the Spirit freely all its operations, and make a free Covenant of grace and mercy to pardon all sin, to receive a sinner into his bosom, *without money or price*; nay not to offer any thing of his own, either Duty, or Righteousness . . . this call Free Grace." *A Dying Fathers Last Legacy*, pp. 58–61.

15. *Free-Grace*, pp. 144, 104.

16. *Christ's Spirit a Christian's Strength*, pp. 35, 43; *Crucified Christian*, p. 352.

17. *The Exaltation of Christ in the Dayes of the Gospel*, 2d ed., p. 251.

18. *Free-Grace*, p. 94.

19. Dell, *Christ's Spirit*, p. 48; Collier, *Exaltation*, p. 144; Dell, *Crucified Christian*, pp. 342–43; Saltmarsh, *A Solemn Discourse*, p. 4.

20. Winthrop S. Hudson, "Mystical Religion in the Puritan Commonwealth," *Journal of Religion*, XXVIII (1948), 51–56. Hudson also suggested that the strain of Puritan mysticism represented by Dell and Saltmarsh (ordained ministers themselves) was primarily lay in spirit (the "mechanicks") and proletarian in social outlook, whereas the other strain was clerical and middle-class. See also Johnson, *Church History*, XVII, 308–10.

21. Haller, *Church History*, XIX, 30–31; *Writings and Speeches*, I, 360, 365.

22. Dell, *Building, Beauty*, p. 92.

23. Firth, *Clarke Papers*, XLIX, 238.

24. *Right Reformation*, p. 130. For Erbury's views, see [Francis Chey-nell], *An Account Given to the Parliament*, p. 14. Saltmarsh wrote in 1647: "There is a ministry of gifts, of teachings, and ordinances . . . for the perfecting of the Saints" (*Sparkles*, p. 126).

25. Collier, *Exaltation*, p. 30; Henry Denne, *The Man of Sinne Discovered*, p. 23; Saltmarsh, *Free-Grace*, p. 130.

26. Samuel Rutherford, *Christ Dying and Drawing Sinners to Himselfe*, "To the Reader."

27. Peters, *A Dying Fathers Last Legacy*, pp. 2, 66. For an ordered presentation of Peters' theological views in 1641, before he became associated with Dell and Saltmarsh in the New Model Army, see his *Milke for Babes, and Meat for Men.* Just before his death Peters professed that he had been "Orthodox in all Points of Religion" according to the Confession of the Westminster Assembly (*A Dying Fathers Last Legacy*, p. 3). For the Federalist influence in the Westminster Assembly see Trinterud, *Church History*, XX, 52.

28. Baxter, *Aphorismes of Justification*, p. 265. Baxter would say neither that good works alone were effectual in bringing justification nor that they brought justification as an equal part with faith. Faith was the principal condition and good works the "secondary lesse-principall" condition of the covenant (*ibid.*, p. 299).

29. *A Conference Between a Sick Man and a Minister*, p. 14.

30. Samuel Richardson, *Justification by Christ Alone*, p. 2.

31. Saltmarsh, *Free-Grace*, pp. 191, 91.

32. *A Mistake, or, Misconstruction, Removed*, p. 24; *Shadowes Without Substance*, p. 13.

33. John Crandon, *Mr. Baxters Aphorisms Exorized and Anthorized*, pp. 271–73; Saltmarsh, *Sparkles*, p. 189; Baxter, *Aphorismes*, p. 111.

34. See Henry Denne, *Grace, Mercy, and Peace*, pp. 75, 69, 43–44: "If I should say, without eating and drinking no man can live; wouldst thou presently conclude, that I must eate and drinke before I be alive? When sense will tell thee I must be alive, before I can eate and drinke." Thomas-Atwood Rotherham (*A Den of Theeves Discovered*, p. 37) accused Denne of blasphemy. "They that are Christs do beleeve, and repent, and obey; but do they *believe, repent,* and *obey* that they may be Christs?" Saltmarsh, *Reasons for Unitie, Peace, and Love*, p. 134.

35. Gataker, *A Mistake*, p. 6; *Shadowes*, p. 11.

36. Collier, *Exaltation*, p. 126; Saltmarsh, *Sparkles*, "To the Reader"; Saltmarsh, *Free-Grace*, p. 74.

37. Rich: *Baxter's Confession of His Faith*, Preface, pp. 3–4.

38. Saltmarsh, *Sparkles*, p. 192; Powicke, *Baxter*, I, 242; Baxter, *The Saints Everlasting Rest*, p. 390.

39. Collier, *Exaltation*, p. 196; Saltmarsh, *Sparkles*, pp. 274–75; Saltmarsh, *Free-Grace*, p. 149.

40. *Writings and Speeches*, I, 416. Saltmarsh dedicated his pamphlet *The Smoke in the Temple* to Lord Say and Sele and Oliver Cromwell, "*who know the* mystery *of the* Spirit *and of* Christ."

41. If any are to be damned, wrote Baxter (*Aphorismes*, pp. 101–4), it must be for breaking either the first or second covenant. If it was the first, one may escape damnation by pleading that the second covenant fulfilled the first. If it was the second covenant, the same plea will hold: i.e., "Christ [has] fulfilled both Covenants for all men"; therefore none can perish. Samuel Rutherford (*A Survey of the Spirituall Antichrist*, Part I, p. 215) also thought Saltmarsh preached universal grace.

42. Saltmarsh, *Free-Grace*, p. 115; Dell, *The Way of True Peace*, pp. 183–84; *A Sermon by Hugh Peters: Preached Before His Death*, pp. 10–11; Erbury, *The Lord of Hosts*, p. 5. Saltmarsh contradicted himself in *Free-Grace* (p. 113) by stating that election and predestination came not before time began, but only when God gave Christ to man.

43. "If you shall place the *Emphasis* of this Text, in *All*, and *Many*, you will cause the hearts of the universall Gratians to leape for joy; which (I beleeve) you would not willingly doe. Therefore you must be forced to place the *Emphasis* in *As*, and *So*: *As* wee sinned all in the loynes of the first Adam, *So* were all made righteous in the loynes of the second *Adam, the Lord Christ*" (Denne, *Grace, Mercy, and Peace*, p. 73).

44. *Free-Grace*, p. 203.

45. *Reasons for Unitie, Peace, and Love*, p. 136.

46. *Free-Grace*, pp. 143, 150, 187, 102, 31.

47. Rutherford, *Christ Dying*, p. 503; Saltmarsh, *Free - Grace*, pp. 202–3.

48. Collier, *The Marrow of Christianity*, pp. 15–16; *The Fountaine of Free Grace Opened by Questions and Answers, passim. The Fountaine of Free Grace Opened* may have been written by Saltmarsh himself, though it differs somewhat from the views stated in *Free-Grace*. Both do oppose universal salvation.

49. *A Mistake*, p. 26.

50. Edwards, *Gangraena*, Part I, pp. 77–78; Erbury, *The Testimony of William Erbery*, p. 264.

51. Denne, *A Conference*, p. 8; Denne, *The Drag-Net of the Kingdome of Heaven*, p. 100; Rutherford, *Christ Dying*, "To the Reader"; Bedford, *An Examination of the Chief Points of Antinomianism*, p. 62.

52. See Haller and Davies, *Leveller Tracts*, pp. 38–40.

53. Baxter, *The Saints Everlasting Rest*, p. 303. "To this day many Antinomian Teachers, who are magnified as the only Preachers of Free Grace, do assert and proclaim, That of the vilest Murderer or Whore-master, but to beleeve that he is justified, or to be perswaded that God loveth him" (Baxter, *Aphorismes of Justification*, p. 330).

54. Gataker, *A Mistake*, p. 20.

55. *Characters and Elegies*, p. 14.

56. *Building, Beauty*, pp. 78–79.

CHAPTER THREE

1. See, for example, Saltmarsh, *The Divine Right of Presbytery*, pp. 108–9, or Collier, *General Epistle*, p. 65; "I cannot but judge some amongst you, to be tender and pretious, although I must confesse, that I looke on that Forme [Presbyterianism], to be one of the lowest where *Christ* may be found."

2. *Uniformity Examined*, pp. 64, 61.

3. *Certaine Queries*, p. 24.

4. *Groanes for Liberty*, p. 85.

5. Woodhouse, *Puritanism and Liberty*, Introduction, pp. 67–68.

6. *XXXII Propositions or Articles Subscribed by Severall Reformed Churches*, p. 3.

7. Rutherford, *A Survey of the Spiritual Antichrist*, Part II, pp. 99–100. Three years earlier Rutherford had written in a much different vein: "if the king refuse to reform religion, the inferior judges and assembly of godly pastors and other church officers may reform; if the king will not . . . do his duty in purging the House of the Lord, may not Eli[j]ah and the people do their duty and cast out Baal's priests?" (*Lex, Rex*, reprinted in Woodhouse, *Puritanism and Liberty*, pp. 199–200).

8. Saltmarsh, *Sparkles*, pp. 165–69.

9. Gardiner, *History of the Great Civil War*, II, 150.

10. Edwards, *Gangraena*, Part III, pp. 121, 125.

11. Saltmarsh, *The Divine Right of Presbytery*, p. 108; Saltmarsh, *The Smoke in the Temple*, p. 20; Collier, *General Epistle*, p. 98.

12. In January 1645, Saltmarsh was located in the rectory of Brasted, Kent. About this time a committee of Parliament authorized Saltmarsh to deliver a lecture at Westerham, but some citizens from that market town and from Brasted threatened to "draw up divers fyles of Musquetires against him." Those in rebellion against Saltmarsh were led by a justice of the peace, who had a large magazine of arms, but Colonel Blunt appeared in behalf of Saltmarsh and there was no trouble. On 29 January 1646 a committee of divines investigated the matter, and Ley, a member of the committee, noted that the Brasted rector with ingenuous modesty proved himself well qualified to be employed in the ministry (Ley, *The New Quere*, p. 1).

13. *Light for Smoke*, p. 46.

14. *Right Reformation*, pp. 117, 155.

15. *Sparkles*, "The Epistle Dedicatory"; Peters took the same position in *Mr. Peter's Last Report*, p. 8, and in *A Word for the Armie*, p. 12.

16. Collier, *Certaine Queries*, p. 5; Dell, *Building, Beauty*, p. 95; Webster, *The Saints Guide*, pp. 32–33.

17. The greatest Erastian work from Prynne's prolific pen was *The Sword of Christian Magistracy Supported*. In this work he exalted the power of the state in order to prove that Parliament was the seat of all authority. See pp. 109, 112.

18. Dell, *Right Reformation*, pp. 131, 158; Prynne, *The Sword of Christian Magistracy*, "The Epistle Dedicatory"; Dell, *Crucified Christian*, p. 317.

19. Prynne, *The Sword of Christian Magistracy*, pp. 120, 101; Dell, *Christ's Spirit*, p. 26.

20. See *Building, Beauty*, pp. 109–11.

21. Collier, *Certaine Queries*, p. 24; Denne, *The Man of Sinne Discovered*, p. 20; Webster, *The Judgement Set*, p. 276, and *The Saints Guide*, p. 28.

22. *Sparkles*, "The Epistle Dedicatory."

23. *Right Reformation*, "Epistle Dedicatory."

24. Woodhouse, *Puritanism and Liberty*, p. 15.

25. *The Platonic Renaissance in England*, pp. 77–78.

26. Dell, *Christ's Spirit*, p. 19.

27. Hobbes, *Leviathan*, chap. xvii, p. 87, quoted in Gertrude Huehns, *Antinomianism in English History*, p. 113 n.

28. Dell, *Right Reformation*, p. 116.

29. Both views, Maitland thought, were erroneous, but the latter was the less dangerous (Frederick William Maitland, *Collected Papers*, III, 22–23).

30. See Dell, *Uniformity Examined*, pp. 58, 64; Saltmarsh, *The Smoke in the Temple*, "Dedication," p. 6; Saltmarsh, *The Divine Right of Presbytery*, pp. 106–7; Dell, *Building, Beauty*, pp. 93, 100–101.

31. *Uniformity Examined*, pp. 60–61.

32. *Building, Beauty*, pp. 70–71; Hudson, *Journal of Religion*, XXVIII, 52.

33. *Writings and Speeches*, I, 377.

34. Wilbur K. Jordan, *The Development of Religious Toleration in England*, III, 145; Maurice Ashley, "Oliver Cromwell: the Spiritual Anarchist," *The Listener*, XLVI (6 September 1951), pp. 373–74. To Rutherford, however, Cromwell's letter was no proof of any inward and spiritual unity within the Army, for there are in the Army "by name *Jo. Saltmarsh*, Mr. *Del*, and Seekers, who in Print disclaime both *Presbyterians* and *Independents*" (*A Survey of the Spirituall Antichrist*, Part I, p. 251).

35. Dell, *Right Reformation*, p. 133, *Building, Beauty*, p. 91; Saltmarsh, *The Smoke in the Temple*, pp. 3, 69–70, *Free-Grace*, p. 150.

36. Saltmarsh, *The Smoke in the Temple*, p. 3, "To the Believers"; Dell, *Building, Beauty*, p. 101; Saltmarsh, *An End of One Controversie*, p. 122.

37. Saltmarsh, *The Smoke in the Temple*, pp. 1-3, 33; Peters, *A Word for the Armie*, p. 11; Saltmarsh, *Dawnings of Light*, pp. 57–58.

38. Dell, *The Way of True Peace*, p. 300; Collier, *Certaine Queries*, p. 26.

39. Milton, *Works*, ed. Frank Allen Patterson, III, 181, 223; IV, 319, 333, 311–12.

40. The same view may be found in William Sedgwick's *Justice upon the Armie Remonstrance*, p. 14.
41. Milton, *Works*, IV, 337–39, 342.
42. *Ibid.*, XIV, 103; XVI, 265–67; VI, 5–6.
43. *The Way of True Peace*, p. 299; *Building, Beauty*, p. 102.
44. Never are perplexity and disquietude quite so much in evidence, wrote Saltmarsh, as when the will of man is in disjuncture with the will of God (*Sparkles*, pp. 154–55).
45. Woodhouse, *Puritanism and Liberty*, pp. 85, 100–101, 104–5, 9, 38.
46. *Building, Beauty*, p. 92.
47. Woodhouse, *Puritanism and Liberty*, pp. 101–8.

CHAPTER FOUR

1. Saltmarsh, *The Smoke in the Temple*, p. 6; Dell, *The Way of True Peace*, p. 305.
2. Peters, *A Word for the Armie*, p. 12; [Nathaniel Ward], *A Word to Mr. Peters*, pp. 36–37.
3. Perry Miller, *Roger Williams*, pp. 114–15.
4. *The Way of True Peace*, p. 300.
5. *Building, Beauty*, p. 155; *Right Reformation*, p. 167.
6. *Short and Plaine Animadversions*, p. 44.
7. *Dawnings of Light*, pp. 38–39; *Sparkles*, 1847 ed., p. 117.
8. Woodhouse, *Puritanism and Liberty*, Introduction, p. 68.
9. Williams, *The Bloudy Tenent of Persecution*, p. 89.
10. *Publications of the Narragansett Club*, IV, 135; *The Bloudy Tenent*, pp. 70–71.
11. This eschatological basis for religious toleration is discussed in Roland Bainton, "The Parable of the Tares," *Church History*, I (1932), 67. It is repeatedly invoked by Williams in *The Bloudy Tenent*.
12. *The Bloudy Tenent*, pp. 115, 222.
13. Michael Freund, "Roger Williams, Apostle of Complete Religious Liberty," trans. James E. Ernst, *Rhode Island Historical Society Collections*, XXVI (1933), 132.
14. Webster, *The Saints Guide*, p. 33; Dell, *The Way of True Peace*, p. 281; Saltmarsh, *A New Quaere*, p. 3.
15. Saltmarsh, *Sparkles*, p. 138; Collier, *General Epistle*, p. 79; Peters, *A Word for the Armie*, p. 12.
16. *The Bloudy Tenent*, pp. 46–47.
17. *Puritanism and Liberty*, Introduction, p. 58.
18. Saltmarsh, *Dawnings of Light*, p. 36; Dell, *The Way of True Peace*, pp. 182–83; Dell, *The Tryal of Spirits*, p. 472.
19. Saltmarsh, *Sparkles*, p. 160.
20. *Ibid.*, p. 304.

21. *The Bloudy Tenent,* p. 214.

22. See *Publications of the Narragansett Club,* II, 135, 249, 343, 364; Williams, *The Bloudy Tenent,* p. 295; James Ernst, *The Political Thought of Roger Williams,* p. 426; *Records of Rhode Island,* I, 156, quoted in Charles Borgeaud, *The Rise of Democracy in Old and New England,* pp. 158–61.

23. Woodhouse, *Puritanism and Liberty,* Introduction, p. 68.

24. *The Way of True Peace,* p. 266; see also *Christ's Spirit,* pp. 22, 33, and *Building, Beauty,* pp. 87, 91, 102.

25. *Salus Electorum,* p. 308.

26. *Walwyns Just Defence,* p. 8, reprinted in Haller and Davies, *Leveller Tracts,* p. 361; William Haller, ed., *Tracts on Liberty in the Puritan Revolution,* I, 41; Walwyn, *A Whisper in the Eare of Mr. Thomas Edwards,* p. 2.

27. Woodhouse, *Puritanism and Liberty,* Introduction, p. 54.

28. A. W. Harrison, *Arminianism,* p. 49; Rutherford, *A Survey of the Spirituall Antichrist,* Part II, p. 57. See also John Crandon, *Mr. Baxters Aphorisms,* pp. 242–43; Thomas Whitfield, *A Refutation,* p. 54.

29. Thomas Edwards has paraphrased the Leveller idea of equality as follows: "That seeing all men are by nature the Sons of Adam, and from him have legitimatly derived a naturall propriety, right, and freedom, Therefore *England* and all other Nations, all particular persons in every Nation, notwithstanding the difference of Lawes and Governments, rancks and degrees, ought to be alike free and estated in their naturall Liberties, and to enjoy the just Rights and Prerogative of mankind, whereunto they are Heirs apparent; and thus the Commoners by right, are equall with the Lords. For by naturall birth all men are equally and alike born to like propriety, liberty, and freedom; and as we are delivered of God by the hand of nature into this world, every one with a naturall innate freedom, and propriety, even so are we to live, every one equally and alike to enjoy his birth-right and priviledge" (*Gangraena,* Part III, p. 17). The substance of this quotation may be found in John Lilburne, *The Free-Mans Freedome Vindicated,* p. 11.

30. In addition, see the earlier covenant of the first Independent Church in England, which was founded in 1616 by Henry Jacob (Horton Davies, *The Worship of the English Puritans,* Appendix C).

31. J. W. Gough (*The Social Contract,* p. 91) has suggested that the Leveller *Agreement of the People* was influenced to some extent by the example of the Scottish National Covenant of 1638. It must not be forgotten that the Army covenanted together in June 1647 not to disband until its rights and liberties were guaranteed.

32. Woodhouse, *Puritanism and Liberty,* pp. 207-8.

33. Baxter, *Reliquiae,* pp. 107-8.

34. *A Holy Commonwealth,* "Preface," pp. 216–17, 221; Schlatter, *Richard Baxter and Puritan Politics,* p. 37.

35. The most distinctive feature of Peters' church at Rotterdam was the procedure he introduced for ordaining the minister of the congregation. After mutual agreement upon a covenant to which the members were required to subscribe (the penalty being excommunication), the minister was "called" by the members. Peters then accepted the "call" and was fully ordained in his new charge by the ceremony of the laying on of hands. This ceremony guaranteed the apostolic succession of the saints, and the Rotterdam congregation became a "true" church. Raymond P. Stearns, *Congregationalism in the Dutch Netherlands*, p 47; Stearns, *The Essex Institute Historical Collections*, LXXII, 47.

36. As for the "bold and blustring brother Peters," wrote one pamphleteer, "I can almost prophecy that Dell and Saltmarsh must be your fellows, you are Birds of a feather" (*Hinc Illae Lachrymae*, p. 20).

37. *The Way of True Peace*, pp. 308, 246, 251.

38. Bastwick, *Utter Routing*, p. 47; Saltmarsh, *The Smoke in the Temple*, pp. 32, 74, 69.

39. Erbury, *Testimony*, pp. 63, 133.

40. *Oliver Cromwell and the Rule of the Puritans in England*, p. 145; for Lilburne's views, see Perez Zagorin, *A History of Political Thought in the English Revolution*, p. 9.

41. Ley, *The New Quere*, p. 95.

42. See Haller and Davies, *Leveller Tracts*, p. 40.

CHAPTER FIVE

1. *Characters and Elegies*, p. 15.

2. Saltmarsh, *Sparkles*, p. 68 (the idea of the three ages can also be found in Joachim of Fiora); Erbury, *Testimony*, pp. 243, 232.

3. Niebuhr, *The Nature and Destiny of Man*, II, 169–70; Dell, *Christ's Spirit*, p. 4; [Saltmarsh], *Wonderfull Predictions*, p. 3; Woodhouse, *Puritanism and Liberty*, p. 138.

4. See, for example, William Sedgwick, *Some Flashes of Lightnings of the Sonne of Man* (London, 1648), p. 88. The following passage from Sedgwick's *Justice Upon the Armie Remonstrance*, written a year later, presents a different view: "When we began the war there was this in our minds, and hath been in our mindes continually, That the King and his party were wicked men, and not worthy or fit for their places and power they had; and that we were Saints, godly, and they did properly belong to us: That the Saints are to have the high places in the earth, and now was the time for these things to be performed, and no body is now fit to administer justice, to rule over men, but we" (p. 23).

5. "Christ is in all *his* in *spirit* and *truth*, and as the *eternal seed*," wrote Saltmarsh in terms suggestive of the Quakers, adding, "all *growth, improvement*, or *reformation* that is to be, is onely the *revelation* or *appearance* of this" (*Sparkles*, pp. 295–96). Saltmarsh used such terms as "Light," "seed

of God," and "candle," all employed by the Quakers. For the connection between Saltmarsh, Dell, and the Quakers, see Rufus Jones, *Studies in Mystical Religion*, pp. 467, 485, 490–91; see Johnson, *Church History*, XVII, 309–15.

6. Saltmarsh, *Sparkles*, pp. 23–24. "Some men thinke to see the *Kingdome* of God comming in such and such a person; to see the Kingdom of God comming in and such sights and voices, these are delusions, Behold the *kingdome* of *Christ, the kingdome of God, the kingdom of heaven is within you*" (Sedgwick, *Some Flashes of Lightnings*, p. 88).

7. *Right Reformation*, p. 159.

8. See *The Lord of Hosts*, p. 25, *Testimony*, pp. 94, 232, 189. Although Erbury said the rule of the saints was only spiritual, the language he used indicated something very literal: "God will so rise and reveal himself in the Saints, that they in his appearance and with his power shall oppose those earthly powers and Kings of the earth, yea imprison and punish with the sword upon the earth" (*Testimony*, p. 31).

9. When Saltmarsh first suggested that the kingdoms of Christ and the world were separate, he promptly expounded upon the wrong endured by the church when the state interfered with it, but had nothing to say about the church should it interfere with the state. Saltmarsh, *Dawnings of Light*, p. 36.

10. *The Way of True Peace*, p. 173; *The Stumbling-Stone*, p. 418.

11. *The Marrow of Christianity*, p. 91; *A Vindication of the Army-Remonstrance*, p. 6. On p. 17, however, Collier observes that although admittedly "Saints rights" are secured in heaven, the saints may lawfully use whatever means God directs them to use for the recovery or preservation of their own just interests.

12. *Sparkles*, p. 159. This is exactly the position that St. Thomas Aquinas and Richard Hooker took. Woodhouse notes that Hooker, in holding this view, rejects the principle of the segregation of grace and nature ("Religion and Some Foundations of English Democracy," *Philosophical Review*, LXI [1952], 513–14).

13. *Dawnings of Light*, "The Epistle."

14. Mauro Calamandrei, "Neglected A s p e c t s of Roger Williams' Thought," *Church History*, XXI (September, 1952), p. 255. There is some evidence of this in Williams' tract, *George Fox Digg'd Out of His Burrowes*, written much later in his lifetime, in which he speaks of the "Kingdome of Christ (so often promised in the future, and to come)" (*Publications of the Narragansett Club*, V, 231).

15. *Writings and Speeches*, IV, 445.

16. "*The Lords People are his portion* on Earth . . . and so he will give *Nations and Kingdoms for them*, and . . . *the Nations and Kingdoms that will not serve thee, shall perish* . . . Oh that this Kingdom in it self, and in its representation, would avoid this evil, as they would escape this end" (Dell, *Building, Beauty*, p. 108).

17. See Niebuhr, *The Nature and Destiny of Man*, II, chap. iv.

18. William Erbury and Francis Cheynell, *Nor Truth, Nor Error, Nor Day, Nor Night*, p. 18.

19. See *Christ's Spirit*, p. 10.

20. [Cheynell], *An Account Given to the Parliament*, pp. 38, 45, 48, 51–52; Erbury and Cheynell, *Nor Truth*, p. 1.

21. *Christ's Spirit*, pp. 14, 35.

22. *Writings and Speeches*, I, 365.

23. Dell, *Building, Beauty*, p. 73; Erbury, *The Lord of Hosts*, p. 14; Peters, *God's Doings*, p. 1.

24. *A Little Eye-Salve for the Kingdome and Armie*, pp. 5–6.

25. *Second View*, pp. 17, 6, 11; *Leaves*, p. 45.

26. Dell, *Building, Beauty*, p. 68; [Dell], *A Vindication*, p. 8; *A Perfect Diurnall of Some Passages in Parliament*, 8–15 February 1647.

27. Lilburne, *A Discourse Betwixt Lieutenant Colonel John Lilburn . . . and Mr. Hugh Peter*; Massey, *The Examination and Correction of a Paper Lately Printed.*

28. John Rushworth, *Historical Collections*, VIII, 662.

29. John Lilburne, *The Grand Plea of Lieut. Col. John Lilburne* (1647), p. 19.

30. *The Perfect Weekly Account*, 10–17 November 1647; *Mercurius Anti-Pragmaticus*, 11–18 November 1647, p. 7; *A Bloody Independent Plot Discovered*, p. 2; *Hampton-Court Conspiracy*, p. 3; *A Remonstrance from His Excellency Sir Thomas Fairfax*, p. 69.

31. John Goodwin, *Right and Might Well Met* (1648); Stearns, *The Strenuous Puritan*, pp. 326, 331, 334; *Calamy Revised, s.v.*

32. *A Perfect Narrative . . . in the Tryal of the King*, p. 11.

33. Actually, this pairing makes more sense than it might appear to make at first glance. It has been pointed out by J. N. Figgis (*Divine Right*, p. 284) that the Leveller concept of a supreme overriding law to which appeals could be made against all civil and ecclesiastical institutions was not unrelated to two other political theories of seventeenth-century England: namely, the Stuart Divine Right of Monarchy and the Scots' Divine Right of Presbytery. The Stuart concept of Divine Right placed the sole authority for the interpretation of God's will in the monarchy; the Presbyterian concept of Divine Right placed the responsibility for ascertaining God's will in the clergy; the Leveller concept of Divine Right rested with the rule of the majority. Legalistically speaking, then, royalists, Presbyterians, and Levellers were in one camp. In the enemy camp were the Antinomians. The Antinomian, with his belief in the goodness of the saints, dismissed law as unnecessary; the Leveller (together with the Presbyterian), viewing man as a creature of sin, claimed that man must be regulated by law.

34. Edwards, *Gangraena*, Part III, p. 112. "Good men may save a Nation, when good Lawes cannot" (*Mr. Peters Message*, p. 2).

35. Rice Vaughan, *A Plea for the Common-Laws of England*, p. 5.
36. *A Word for the Armie*, p. 8.
37. *Ibid.*, p. 3.
38. Vaughan, *A Plea*, "An Introduction"; *Good Work for a Good Magistrate*, p. 37.
39. J. R. Tanner, ed., *Constitutional Documents of the Reign of James I*, pp. 340–41.
40. Francis Wormuth, *The Royal Prerogative, 1603–1649*, p. 78; George L. Mosse, *The Holy Pretence*, p. 14.
41. *Mr. Peter's Last Report*, p. 6; Peters, *A Word for the Armie*, pp. 5, 7.
42. Cook, *Redintegratio Amoris*, p. 68; Baillie, *Letters*, III, 16; Saltmarsh, *A Letter from the Army*, pp. 3–4.
43. Collier, *A Vindication*, p. 28; Edwards, *Gangraena*, Part III, p. 146; *Mr. Peter's Last Report*, p. 7; Woodhouse, *Puritanism and Liberty*, p. 135. In *Anglia Rediviva* Sprigge had written "there is the best policy where there is the best piety" (p. 323), as a tribute to the character of General Fairfax for surrounding himself with advisers who had a religious reputation.
44. *Practice of Policie*, pp. 2, 7, 11, 27, 31, 48, 149.
45. *Examinations, or a Discovery of Some Dangerous Positions*, p. 4.
46. *The Smoke in the Temple*, pp. 26, 53.
47. See Margaret Judson, *The Crisis of the Constitution*, pp. 7–8.
48. *A Letter from the Army*, p. 4. "Indeed formerly I was a stickler in *Yorkshire* for the *Parliament*; but I have been since taught (I blesse God) onely to pray for them and obey them."
49. *A Solemn Discourse*, p. 7.
50. *Examinations*, p. 6.
51. *The Smoke in the Temple*, p. 30.
52. *Examinations*, p. 7.
53. *A Solemn Discourse*, p. 7.

CHAPTER SIX

1. See Petegorsky, *Left-Wing Democracy*, p. 24.
2. *Religion and the Rise of Capitalism*, Mentor ed., p. 168.
3. *Ibid.*, pp. 201–2; Winthrop S. Hudson, "Puritanism and the Spirit of Capitalism," *Church History*, XVIII (1949), 9, 13.
4. *The Saints Fulnesse of Joy*, p. 32.
5. Petegorsky, *Left-Wing Democracy*, pp. 64–65; the point about universal salvation is, as we have seen, untenable. See also Charles H. George, "A Social Interpretation of English Puritanism," *Journal of Modern History*, XXV (1953), 341. George concluded that the "frightening independency" of the Army was a religion of the poor (which to some extent is true) and a religion of the damned (which is quite incorrect).

6. Peters, *God's Doings*, p. 41; Dell, *Right Reformation*, p. 158; Dell, *Building, Beauty*, p. 87.

7. *Mr. Peter's Last Report*, p. 9. However, Peters felt that merchants should be encouraged with a Law of Merchants.

8. *Building, Beauty*, p. 91.

9. Woodhouse, *Puritanism and Liberty*, p. 57.

10. *The Lord of Hosts*, p. 25.

11. "English Puritanism and Its Importance in Schemes of Legal and Social Reform," a lecture delivered on 10 July 1951 at the Oxford Arts Festival, Oxford, England.

12. Robert Baillie, *Anabaptism, the True Fountaine*, Preface. John Bastwick wrote that many of the "Independent itinerary preachers run from place to place, preaching against the Nobility and Gentry, against the Reverend Assembly, against the Directory, against Tythes, against the Presbytery; yea against all that is called authority" (*Utter Routing*, "The Epistle to the Reader").

13. Petegorsky, *Left-Wing Democracy*, p. 65; Firth, *Cromwell's Army*, p. 40.

14. D. B. Robertson has discussed at some length the "anti-intellectual" views of John Spencer and Samuel How, two "mechanick" preachers (*The Religious Foundations of Leveller Democracy*, pp. 33–37). The following title of a pamphlet by How is suggestive: *The Sufficiencie of the Spirits Teaching Without Human Learning: or, a Treatise Tending to Prove Humane Learning to Be no Help to the Spiritual Understanding of the Word of God*.

15. Dell, *The Tryal of Spirits*, pp. 554, 635. Furthermore, wrote Dell, the universities have kept the same "forms and follies," such as hoods, caps, scarlet robes, doctoral ring and dinner, and music. In Tudor times as well as during the ascendancy of Archbishop Laud, some of these forms had been objects of abuse by the Puritans.

16. *Academiarum Examen*, pp. 4, 9–11, 6–7. Accused of Leveller sympathies, Webster replied, "I must needs so far own Levelling that I hold plain dealing to be a jewel" (*ibid.*, "Epistle to the Reader").

17. Dell, *The Tryal of Spirits*, p. 529; Dell, *Christ's Spirit*, p. 22; Saltmarsh, *An End of One Controversie*, p. 115; Woodhouse, *Puritanism and Liberty*, p. 182.

18. Robertson, *The Religious Foundations of Leveller Democracy*, p. 39.

19. *The Works of Gerrard Winstanley*, p. 238.

20. [Cheynell], *An Account Given to the Parliament*, p. 38.

21. [William Walwyn], *The Power of Love*, p. 44; Dell, *The Tryal of Spirits*, pp. 583, 589.

22. Dell, *The Tryal of Spirits*, pp. 645–48. This secularization of university studies can also be found in Winstanley's *The Law of Freedom* (see *The Works of Gerrard Winstanley*, p. 67).

23. *Reliquiae,* p. 64.

24. *A Word for the Armie,* p. 11. Peters thought that Bacon's *Advancement of Learning* had propounded many excellent and "learned Problemes, experiments and speculations" (*Good Work for a Good Magistrate,* pp. 74–75).

25. See W. A. L. Vincent, *The State and School Education, 1640–1660, in England and Wales,* p. 88.

26. *Every Mans Right,* pp. 5–6.

27. Collier, *A Discovery of the New Creation,* p. 35; Ogg, Oxford Arts Festival lecture, 10 July 1951.

28. *A Word for the Armie,* p. 13.

29. See Richard Overton, *An Appeale,* reprinted in Don M. Wolfe, ed., *Leveller Manifestoes of the Puritan Revolution,* pp. 192–93.

30. He asked "That all Lawes of the Land (lockt up from common capacities in the Latine or French tongues,) may bee translated into the English tongue" (*A Discovery of the New Creation,* p. 35).

31. *Mercurius Populi,* [11 November 1647], p. 5, quoted in Schenk, *The Concern for Social Justice,* p. 67; Peters, *A Word for the Armie,* pp. 12–13.

32. Massey, *The Examination and Correction of a Paper Lately Printed.*

33. Peters, *Good Work for a Good Magistrate,* pp. 32–33; *The Works of Gerrard Winstanley,* p. 509.

34. *Memorials,* III, 388.

35. *The Works of Gerrard Winstanley,* p. 238.

36. See Margaret James, "Political Importance of the Tithes Controversy," *History,* XXVII (1941), 9-11.

37. Collier, *A Discovery of the New Creation,* pp. 36–37, *A Brief Discovery,* pp. 6–7; Saltmarsh, *An End of One Controversie,* p. 115, *The Smoke in the Temple,* p. 36; *Calamy Revised, s.v.; Mercurius Elencticus,* 29 October–5 November 1647, p. 4.

38. *The Stumbling-Stone,* p. 378.

Bibliography

The first six works listed below are bibliographical aids. The remaining items are listed alphabetically, by author's or editor's name wherever possible. Newspapers, public documents, and anonymous works are listed alphabetically by title. Place of publication is London unless otherwise indicated.

Abbott, Wilbur Cortez. A Bibliography of Oliver Cromwell, a List of Printed Materials Relating to Oliver Cromwell, Together with a List of Portraits and Caricatures. Cambridge, Mass., 1929.

Davies, Godfrey, ed. Bibliography of British History, Stuart Period, 1603–1714. Oxford, 1928.

Fortescue, G. K., ed. Catalogue of the Pamphlets, Books, Newspapers, and Manuscripts Relating to the Civil War, the Commonwealth, and Restoration Collected by George Thomason, 1640–1661. 2 vols., 1908.

Gillett, Charles R., ed. Catalogue of the McAlpin Collection of British History and Theology. 5 vols. New York, 1927–30.

Pollard, Alfred W., and G. R. Redgrave, et al. A Short-Title Catalogue of Books Printed in England, Scotland, & Ireland and of English Books Printed Abroad, 1475–1640. 1926.

Wing, Donald G. Short-Title Catalogue of Books Printed in England, Scotland, Ireland, Wales, and British America, and of English Books Printed in Other Countries, 1641–1700. 3 vols. New York, 1945.

Adams, Charles Francis, ed. Antinomianism in the Colony of Massachusetts Bay, 1636–1638. Publications of the Prince Society. Boston. 1894.

An Admonition Given unto Mr. Saltmarsh. 1646.

Anti-Machiavell, or, Honesty Against Policy. N.p., 1647.

Ashley, Maurice. Cromwell's Generals. 1954.

———. England in the Seventeenth Century (1603–1714). "The Pelican History of England." 1951.

———. The Greatness of Oliver Cromwell. New York, 1958.

———. John Wildman, Plotter and Postmaster. 1947.

———. "Oliver Cromwell: The Spiritual Anarchist," *The Listener*, XLVI (6 September 1951), 373–74.

Augustine, Saint. The City of God. Translated by John Healey. Edited by R. V. G. Tasker. Everyman's Library. 2 vols. 1947.

Baillie, Robert. Anabaptism, the True Fountaine. 1647.

———. The Letters and Journals of Robert Baillie. Edited by David Laing. 3 vols., Edinburgh, 1841–42.

Bainton, Roland. "The Parable of the Tares as the Proof Text for Religious Liberty to the End of the Sixteenth Century," *Church History*, I (1932), 67–89.

Barclay, Robert. Inner Life of the Religious Societies of the Commonwealth. 1876.

Barker, Arthur. Milton and the Puritan Dilemma, 1641–1660. Toronto, 1942.

Baron, Hans. "Calvinist Republicanism and Its Historical Roots," *Church History*, VIII (1939), 30–42.

Bastwick, John. The Utter Routing of the Whole Army of All the Independents & Sectaries. 1646.

Baxter, Richard. Aphorismes of Justification, with Their Explication Annexed. 1649.

———. A Holy Commonwealth, or Political Aphorisms. 1659.

[———]. A Plea for Congregationall Government: or, a Defence of the Assemblies Petition, Against Mr. John Saltmarsh. 1646.

———. Reliquiae Baxterianae. 1696.

———. Rich: Baxter's Confession of His Faith. 1655.

———. The Saints Everlasting Rest: or, a Treatise of the Blessed State of the Saints in their Enjoyment of God in Glory. 1650.

Bedford, Thomas. An Examination of the Chief Points of Antinomianism. 1647.

Bernstein, Eduard. Cromwell and Communism. Translated by H. J. Stenning. 1930.

A Bloody Independent Plot Discovered. N.p., 1647.

Borgeaud, Charles. The Rise of Democracy in Old and New England. 1894.

Brauer, Jerald C. "Puritan Mysticism and the Development of Liberalism," *Church History*, XIX (1950), 151–70.

———. "Reflections on the Nature of English Puritanism," *Church History*, XXIII (1954), 99–108.

Brown, Louise Fargo. The Political Activities of the Baptists and Fifth Monarchy Men in England During the Interregnum. Washington: American Historical Association, 1912.

Buchan, John. Oliver Cromwell. 1934.

Burrage, Champlin. The Early English Dissenters in the Light of Recent Research. Cambridge, England, 1912.

Burrell, Sidney A. "A Study in the Scottish Backgrounds of the English Civil Wars." Unpublished doctoral dissertation, Columbia University, 1953.

Bush, Douglas. The Renaissance and English Humanism. Toronto. 1939.

Calamandrei, Mauro. "Neglected Aspects of Roger Williams' Thought," *Church History*, XXI (1952), 239–58.

Calamy Revised. Edited by A. G. Matthews. Oxford, 1934.

Calder, Isabel M. "A Seventeenth Century Attempt to Purify the Anglican Church," *American Historical Review*, LIII (1948), 760–75.

Calendar of State Papers (Venetian).

A Case for the City-Spectacles. N.p., 1648.

Cassirer, Ernst. The Platonic Renaissance in England. Translated by James P. Pettegrove. 1953.

[Cheynell, Francis]. An Account Given to the Parliament by the Ministers Sent by Them to Oxford. 1647.

The Cleere Sense: or, a Just Vindication of the Late Ordinance of Parliament. 1645.

Cohn, Norman. The Pursuit of the Millennium. Fairlawn, N.J., 1957.

Collier, Thomas. A Brief Discovery of the Corruption of the Ministrie of the Church of England. 1647.

———. Certaine Queries: or, Points Now in Controvercy. N.p., 1645.

————. A Discovery of the New Creation. In a Sermon Preached at the Head-Quarters at Putney Sept. 29, 1647. 1647.

————. The Exaltation of Christ in the Dayes of the Gospel. 1647.

————. A General Epistle to the Universall Church of the First Born: Whose Names Are Written in Heaven. 1648.

————. The Glory of Christ, and the Ruine of Anti-christ. N.p., 1647.

————. The Marrow of Christianity: or, a Spirituall Discovery of Some Principles of Truth . . . Whereunto Is Added an Epistle, Written by M. Saltmarsh. 1647.

————. A Vindication of the Army-Remonstrance. [1648].

Commons' Journals.

Cook, John. Redintegratio Amoris, or a Union of Hearts. 1647.

Cotton, John. The Covenant of Gods Free Grace. 1645.

Couling, Nicholas. The Saints Perfect in This Life; or Never. 1647.

Cradock, Walter. The Saints Fulnesse of Joy in Their Fellowship with God. 1646.

Crandon, John. Mr. Baxters Aphorisms Exorized and Anthorized. 1654.

Cremeans, Charles D. The Reception of Calvinistic Thought in England. Urbana, Ill., 1949.

Cromwell, Oliver. The Writings and Speeches of Oliver Cromwell. Edited by Wilbur Cortez Abbott. 4 vols. Cambridge, Mass., 1937–47.

[Cromwell, Oliver, and Hugh Peters]. A Coppie of Lieut. Gen. Cromwels Letter: Concerning the Taking of Winchester Castle . . . Together, with Mr. Peters Report Made to the House of Commons, from Lieutenant Gen. Cromwell. 1645.

The Cuckoo's-Nest at Westminster. By Mercurius Melancholicus. N.p., 1648.

Davies, Godfrey. "Arminian versus Puritan in England, *ca.* 1620–1640," *Huntington Library Bulletin,* No. 5 (1934), 157–77.

————. "The Army of the Eastern Association, 1644–5," *English Historical Review,* XLVI (1931), 88–96.

————. The Early Stuarts. "The Oxford History of England." Oxford, 1937.

——. "The Parliamentary Army under the Earl of Essex, 1642–5," *English Historical Review*, XLIX (1934), 32–54.

Davies, Godfrey, *et al*. "The Renaissance Conference at the Huntington Library," *Huntington Library Quarterly*, IV (1941), 133–89.

Davies, Horton. The English Free Churches. 1952.

——. The Worship of the English Puritans. Westminster, 1948.

Dell, William. The Building, Beauty, Teaching and Establishment of the Truly Christian and Spiritual Church. 1651. Printed earlier as The Building and Glory of the Christian Church. 1646. Contained in Several Sermons and Discourses of William Dell. Reprinted in 1709.

——. Christ's Spirit a Christian's Strength. 1651. Printed earlier as Power from on High: or, the Power of the Holy Ghost. 1645. Contained in Several Sermons and Discourses of William Dell. Reprinted in 1709.

——. The Crucified and Quickned Christian. 1651. Contained in Several Sermons and Discourses of William Dell. Reprinted in 1709.

——. Right Reformation, or, the Reformation of the Church of the New-Testament. 1651. Contained in Several Sermons and Discourses of William Dell. Reprinted in 1709.

——. The Stumbling-Stone. 1653.

——. The Tryal of Spirits, Both in Teachers and Hearers. 1666. Contained in Several Sermons and Discourses of William Dell. Reprinted in 1709.

——. Uniformity Examined. 1651. Contained in Several Sermons and Discourses of William Dell. Reprinted in 1709.

[——]. A Vindication of Certain Citizens That Lately Went to the Leaguer, Then Before Oxford. 1646.

——. The Way of True Peace and Unity in the True Church of Christ. 1651. Contained in Several Sermons and Discourses of William Dell. Reprinted in 1709.

Denne, Henry. Antichrist Unmasked in Two Treatises. N.p., 1645.

[——]. An Antidote Against Antinomianisme. [1643].

——. A Conference Between a Sick Man and a Minister, Shewing the Nature of Presumption, Despair, and the True Living Faith. 1643.

——. The Doctrine and Conversation of John Baptist: Delivered in a Sermon. 1643.

——. The Drag-Net of the Kingdome of Heaven: or Christ Drawing All Men. Contained in Antichrist Unmasked in Three Treatises. 1946.

——. Grace, Mercy, and Peace. [1640].

——. The Levellers Designe Discovered. 1649.

——. The Man of Sinne Discovered. 1645.

D'ewes, Simond. The Journal of Sir Simond D'ewes, from the First Recess of the Long Parliament to the Withdrawal of King Charles from London. Edited by Willson Havelock Coates. New Haven, 1952.

Don Pedro De Quixot or in English the Right Reverend Hugh Peters. 1660.

Eaton, John. The Honey-Combe of Free Justification by Christ Alone. 1642.

Edwards, Thomas. Gangraena: or a Catalogue and Discovery of Many of the Errours, Heresies, Blasphemies and Pernicious Practices of the Sectaries of This Time. 1646.

——. The Second Part of Gangraena. 1646.

——. The Third Part of Gangraena. 1646.

Elmen, Paul. "The Theological Basis of Digger Communism," *Church History*, XXXII (1954), 207–18.

Emerson, Everett H. "Calvin and Covenant Theology," *Church History*, XXV (1956), 136–44.

Erbury, William. The Grand Oppressor, or, the Terror of Tithes. 1653.

——. The Lord of Hosts: or, God Guarding the Camp of the Saints, and the Beloved City. 1648.

——. The Testimony of William Erbery, Left upon Record for the Saints of Succeeding Ages. N.p., 1658.

Erbury, William, and Francis Cheynell. Nor Truth, Nor Error, Nor Day, Nor Night. N.p., 1647.

Ernst, James E. The Political Thought of Roger Williams. University of Washington Publications in Language and Literature. Vol. VI, No. 1 (March, 1929).

Eusden, John Dykstra. Puritans, Lawyers, and Politics in Early Seventeenth Century England. New Haven, 1958.

An Extract of Certain Papers of Intelligence, from Cambridge Concerning His Majestie and the Armie. N.p., 1647.

[Fairfax, Sir Thomas]. A Remonstrance from His Excellency Sir Thomas Fairfax. 1647.

[Fairfax, Sir Thomas, and Hugh Peters], Sir Thomas Fairfax Letter to Both Houses of Parliament: More Exactly and Fully Relating the Storming and Taking of Dartmouth . . . Sent by Mr. Peters. 1646.

Figgis, John Neville. The Theory of the Divine Right of Kings. Cambridge, England, 1914.

Firth, Charles H., ed. Clarke Papers. Camden Society Publications. New Series. 4 vols., 1891–1901.

———. Cromwell's Army. 2d ed. 1912.

———. Oliver Cromwell and the Rule of the Puritans in England. 1901.

Firth, Charles H., and Godfrey Davies. The Regimental History of Cromwell's Army. 2 vols. Oxford, 1940.

Firth, Charles H., and Robert S. Rait, eds. Acts and Ordinances of the Interregnum, 1642-1660. 3 vols. 1911.

Foster, Herbert D. Collected Papers. Privately printed, 1929.

The Fountaine of Free Grace Opened by Questions and Answers. London, 1645.

Fourteen Strange Prophesies. N.p., 1648.

Frank, Joseph. The Levellers, a History of the Writings of Three Seventeenth Century Social Democrats: John Lilburne, Richard Overton, and William Walwyn. Cambridge, Mass., 1955.

[Frese, James]. Every Mans Right: or, Englands Perspective-Glasse. N.p. 1646.

Freund, Michael. "Roger Williams, Apostle of Complete Religious Liberty," translated by James E. Ernst, *Rhode Island Historical Society Collections*, XXVI (1932), 101–33.

Friedrich, Carl J. Constitutional Reason of State. Providence, R.I., 1957.

Fuller, Thomas. The Worthies of England. Edited and abridged with an introduction and notes by John Freeman. 1952.

Gardiner, Samuel R. History of England from the Accession of James I to the Outbreak of the Civil War, 1603–1642. New ed. 10 vols. 1893–95.

———. History of the Great Civil War, 1642–1649. 3 vols. 1886–91.

———. Oliver Cromwell. 1901.

Gataker, Thomas. A Mistake, or, Misconstruction, Removed. 1646.

———. Shadowes Without Substance, or, Pretended New Lights. 1646.

George, Charles H. "A Social Interpretation of English Puritanism," *Journal of Modern History,* XXV (1953), 327–42.

Geree, Stephen. The Doctrine of the Antinomians. 1644.

Gibb, M. A. John Lilburne the Leveller, a Christian Democrat. 1947.

Gooch, G. P. English Democratic Ideas in the Seventeenth Century. 2d ed. with notes by H. J. Laski. Cambridge, England, 1927.

Goodman, Christopher. How Superior Powers Ought to Be Obeyed of Their Subjects. Geneva, 1558.

Goodwin, John. Right and Might Well Met. 1648.

G[orton], S[amuel]. Saltmarsh Returned from the Dead. 1655.

Gough, J. W. Fundamental Law in English Constitutional History. Oxford, 1955.

———. The Social Contract. Oxford, 1936.

Haller, William. Liberty and Reformation in the Puritan Revolution. New York, 1955.

———. The Rise of Puritanism. New York, 1938.

———. "The Word of God in the New Model Army," *Church History,* XIX (1950), 15–33.

Haller, William, ed. Tracts on Liberty in the Puritan Revolution, 1638–1647. 3 vols. New York, 1934.

Haller, William, and Godfrey Davies, eds. The Leveller Tracts, 1647–1653. New York, 1944.

Hallowell, John H. The Moral Foundation of Democracy. Chicago, 1954.

Hampton-Court Conspiracy, with the Downfall of the Agitators and Levellers. N.p., 1647.

Harrison, A. W., Arminianism. 1937.

Hassal, George. The Designe of God in the Saints. 1648.

Hexter, J. H. "The Problem of the Presbyterian Independents," *American Historical Review,* XLIV (1938), 29–49.

———. The Reign of King Pym. Harvard Historical Studies. Vol. XLVIII. Cambridge, Mass., 1941.

Hinc Illae Lachrymae or the Impietie of Impunitie. 1648.

Hobson, Paul. A Garden Inclosed, and Wisdom Justified Only of Her Children. 1647.

——. Practicall Divinity. N.p., 1646.

Holorenshaw, Henry. The Levellers and the English Revolution. 1939.

Hudson, Winthrop S. "Economic and Social Thought of Gerrard Winstanley: Was He a Seventeenth-Century Marxist?" *Journal of Modern History*, XVIII (1946), 1–21.

——. "Gerrard Winstanley and the Early Quakers," *Church History*, XII (1943), 177–94.

——. John Ponet (1516?–1556), Advocate of Limited Monarchy. Chicago, 1942.

——. "Mystical Religion in the Puritan Commonwealth," *Journal of Religion*, XXVIII (1948), 51–56.

——. "Puritanism and the Spirit of Capitalism," *Church History*, XVIII (1949), 3–17.

——. "Theological Convictions and Democratic Government," *Theology Today*, X (1953), 230–39.

Huehns, Gertrude. Antinomianism in English History. 1951.

Hyde, Edward, Earl of Clarendon. The History of the Rebellion and Civil Wars in England. 7 vols. Oxford, 1849.

James, Margaret. "The Political Importance of the Tithes Controversy in the English Revolution, 1640–1660," *History*, XXVI (1941), 1–18.

Johnson, George A. "From Seeker to Finder." Unpublished doctoral dissertation, University of Chicago, 1948.

——. "From Seeker to Finder: a Study in Seventeenth Century English Spiritualism Before the Quakers," *Church History*, XVII (1948), 299–315.

Jones, Rufus M. Mysticism and Democracy in the English Commonwealth. Cambridge, Mass., 1932.

——. Studies in Mystical Religion. 1919.

Jordan, Wilbur K. The Development of Religious Toleration in England. 4 vols. 1932–40.

——. "Sectarian Thought and Its Relation to the Development of Religious Toleration, 1640–1660," *Huntington Library Quarterly*, III (1939–40), 294–308.

Jubbes, John. An Apology unto the . . . Officers of . . . the Lord Generals Army. N.p., 1649.

Judson, Margaret. The Crisis of the Constitution. New Brunswick, N.J., 1949.

A Key to the Cabinet of the Parliament by Their Remembrancer. N.p., 1648.

The Kingdomes Weekly Intelligencer. 3–10 August 1647.

Knappen, M. M. Tudor Puritanism, A Chapter in the History of Idealism. Chicago, 1939.

L[ane], S[amuel]. A Vindication of Free-Grace. 1645.

Laud, William. The Works of . . . William Laud, Sometime Lord Archbishop of Canterbury. Edited by William Scott and James Bliss. 7 in 9 vols. Oxford, 1847–60.

Lewin, John. The Man-Child Brought Forth in Us: or God Manifest in Flesh. [1648].

[Ley, John]. An After-Reckoning with Mr. Saltmarsh. 1646.

——. Light for Smoke: or, a Cleare and Distinct Reply by John Ley. 1646.

——. The New Quere, and Determination upon It. 1646.

The Life and Death of Mr. Vavasor Powell. N.p., 1671.

Lilburne, John. A Discourse Betwixt Lieutenant Colonel John Lilburn Close Prisoner in the Tower of London, and Mr. Hugh Peter: upon May 25, 1649. 1649.

——. The Free-Mans Freedome Vindicated. 1646.

——. The Grand Plea of Lieut. Col. John Lilburne. N.p., 1647.

——. The Peoples Prerogative and Privileges. 1647.

Lindsay, A. D. The Modern Democratic State. 1943.

A Little Eye-Salve for the Kingdome and Armie, That They May See. [London], 1647.

Lord's Journals.

Love, Christopher. A Cleare and Necessary Vindication of the Principles and Practices of Me Christopher Love. N.p., 1651.

——. Short and Plaine Animadversions on Some Passages in Mr. Dels Sermon. 1646.

McIlwain, Charles H. Constitutionalism, Ancient and Modern. Ithaca, N.Y., 1947.

McLachlan, H. John. Socinianism in Seventeenth-Century England. Oxford, 1951.

Maclean, A. H. "George Lawson and John Locke," *Cambridge Historical Journal,* IX (1947), 69–77.

Maclear, James Fulton. "The Birth of the Free Church Tradition," *Church History,* XXVI (1957), 99–131.

Maitland, Frederick William. Collected Papers. Edited by H. A. L. Fisher. 3 vols. Cambridge, England, 1911.

Massey, Robert. The Examination and Correction of a Paper Lately Printed Intituled a Relation of the Discourse Between Mr. Hugh Peters and Lieut. Collonel John Lilborn in the Tower of London. 1649.

Maynwaring, Roger. Religion and Alegiance: in Two Sermons Preached Before the Kings Majestie. 1627.

Mercurius Anti-Pragmaticus. 11–18 November 1647.

Mercurius Elencticus. 29 October–5 November 1647. 19–26 November 1647. 12–19 January 1648.

Mercurius Melancholicus. 18–25 December 1647. 15–22 January 1648.

Mercurius Pragmaticus. 16–23 November 1647. 11–18 January 1648. 22–29 May 1649.

Miller, Perry. "The Marrow of Puritan Divinity," *Transactions,* November 1934–February 1935, from the Publications of the Colonial Society of Massachusetts, XXXII (Boston, 1936), 247–300.

——. The New England Mind from Colony to Province. Cambridge, Mass., 1953.

——. The New England Mind, the Seventeenth Century. New York, 1939.

——. Orthodoxy in Massachusetts, 1630–1650. Cambridge, Mass., 1933.

——. Roger Williams: His Contribution to the American Tradition. "Makers of the American Tradition Series." Indianapolis, Ind., 1953.

Milton, John. The Works of John Milton. General editor, Frank Allen Patterson. 18 vols. in 21, New York, 1931–38.

The Moderate Intelligencer, 22–29 January 1646.

Morison, Samuel Eliot. "Sir Charles Firth and Master Hugh Peter with a Hugh Peter Bibliography." *The Harvard Graduates' Magazine,* XXXIX (1930), 121–40.

Morris, Christopher. Political Thought in England from Tyndale to Hooker. 1953.

Mosse, George L. The Holy Pretence, A Study in Christianity and Reason of State from William Perkins to John Winthrop. Oxford, 1957.

———. "Puritanism and Reason of State in Old and New England," *William and Mary Quarterly*, IX (1952), 67–80.

———. The Struggle for Sovereignty in England from the Reign of Queen Elizabeth to the Petition of Right. East Lansing, Mich., 1950.

Nedham, Marchamont. The Case of the Kingdom Stated. 1647.

[———]. Independencie No Schisme. 1646.

Nichols, James Hastings. Democracy and the Churches. Philadelphia, 1951.

Niebuhr, Helmut Richard. The Social Sources of Denominationalism. New York, 1929.

Niebuhr, Reinhold. The Children of Light and the Children of Darkness. New York. 1944.

———. Christian Realism and Political Problems. New York, 1953.

———. The Nature and Destiny of Man. 2 vols. in 1. New York, 1945.

Nineteen Cases of Conscience. Submissively Tendred to Mr. Hugh Peters. 1659.

The Northerne Intelligencer: Communicating the Affayres of Those Parts; and Particularly, the Agitations of Mr. Hugh Peeters. N.p., 1648.

Nuttall, Geoffrey. The Holy Spirit in Puritan Faith and Experience. Oxford, 1946.

———. Visible Saints, The Congregational Way, 1640–1660. Oxford, 1957.

———. The Welsh Saints, 1640–1660, Walter Cradock, Vavasor Powell, Morgan Llwyd. Cardiff, 1957.

Ogg, David. "English Puritanism and Its Importance in Schemes of Legal and Social Reform." A lecture delivered on 10 July 1951 at the Oxford Arts Festival, Oxford, England.

Orders and Instructions from the Lords of the Kings Majesties Privie Councell. 1646.

Owen, John. Salus Electorum. 1648.

Patrick, J. Max. Hugh Peters, a Study in Puritanism. The University of Buffalo Studies. Vol. XVII, No. 4 (March, 1946), pp. 137–207.

Paul, Robert S. The Lord Protector, Religion and Politics in the Life of Oliver Cromwell. 1955.

Peacock, Edward, ed. The Army Lists of the Roundheads and Cavaliers. 1863.

Pease, Theodore Calvin. The Leveller Movement. Washington: American Historical Association, 1916.

A Perfect Diurnall of Some Passages in Parliament. 26 January–2 February 1646. 16–23 March 1646. 8–15 February 1647. 7–14 June 1647. 20–27 December 1647. 13–20 March 1648.

A Perfect Narrative . . . in the Tryal of the King. 1648.

Perfect Occurrences of Both Houses of Parliament and Martiall Affairs. 22–29 May 1646. 5–12 June 1646.

Perfect Occurrences of Every Daies Journall in Parliament. 26 November–3 December 1647.

The Perfect Weekly Account. 10–17 November 1647.

Perfume Against the Sulpherous Stinke of the Snuffe of the Light for Smoak, Called, Novello-Mastix. 1646.

Perry, Ralph Barton. Puritanism and Democracy. New York, 1944.

Petegorsky, David W. Left-Wing Democracy in the English Civil War. 1940.

Peters, Hugh. The Case of Mr. Hugh Peters. [1660].

——. A Dying Fathers Last Legacy to an Only Child. Boston, 1717.

[——]. The Full and Last Relation, of All Things Concerning Basing-House. 1645.

——. God's Doings, and Man's Duty. 2d ed. 1645.

——. Good Work for a Good Magistrate. 1651.

[——]. Master Peters Messuage from Sir Thomas Fairfax. 1646.

——. Milke for Babes, and Meat for Men. 1641.

——. Mr. Peter's Last Report of the English Wars. 1646.

[——]. Mr. Peters Message . . . with the Narration of the Taking of Dartmouth. 1646.

[——]. Mr. Peters Report from the Army, to the Parliament. 1645.

[——]. Mr. Peters Report from Bristol, Made to the House of Commons, from Sir Thomas Fairfax. 1645.

[——]. A Sermon by Hugh Peters: Preached Before His Death. 1660.

[——]. Severall Propositions Presented to the Members of the Honourable House of Commons, by Mr. Peters. 1646.

——. A Word for the Armie. And Two Words to the Kingdome. 1647.

Pinnell, Henry. Nil Novi. This Years Fruit, from the Last Years Root. 1655.

——. A Word of Prophesy, Concerning the Parliament, Generall, and the Army. N.p., 1648.

Powicke, Frederick J. A Life of the Reverend Richard Baxter, 1615–1691. 2 vols. 1924.

Proceedings of the Massachusetts Historical Society. First Series. 20 vols. Boston, 1791–1883.

Prynne, William. A Briefe Justification of the XI. Accused Members. 1647.

[——]. VIII Queries upon the Late Declarations of, and Letters from, the Army. 1647.

——. A Fresh Discovery of Some Prodigious New Wandring-Blasing Stars, & Firebrands. 1645.

[——]. Minors No Senators. 1646.

——. The Sword of Christian Magistracy Supported. 1647.

——. Truth Triumphing over Falsehood, Antiquity over Novelty. 1645.

Ram, Robert. A Sermon Preached at Balderton, March 27, 1646. 1646.

——. The Soldier's Catechisme. N.p., 1644.

Richardson, Samuel. Justification by Christ Alone. 1647.

Robertson, D. B. The Religious Foundations of Leveller Democracy. New York, 1951.

Rotherham, Thomas-Atwood. A Den of Theeves Discovered. 1643.

Rushworth, John. Historical Collections. 8 vols. 1721.

Rutherford, Samuel. Christ Dying and Drawing Sinners to Himselfe. 1647.

——. A Survey of the Spirituall Antichrist. Two parts. 1648.

Salmon, Joseph. Antichrist in Man: or a Discovery of the Great Whore That Sits upon Many Waters. 1648.

Saltmarsh, John. Dawnings of Light: Wherein the True Interest of Reformation Is Opened. 1644.

——. The Divine Right of Presbytery. 1646. Contained in Some Drops of the Viall. 1646.

——. An End of One Controversie. 1646. Contained in Some Drops of the Viall. 1646.

[——]. Englands Friend Raised from the Grave. 1649.

——. Examinations, or a Discovery of Some Dangerous Positions. 1643.

——. Free-Grace; or, the Flowings of Christs Blood Freely to Sinners. Corrected 2d ed. 1646.

——. Groanes for Liberty. 1646. Contained in Some Drops of the Viall. 1646.

——. Holy Discoveries and Flames. 1640.

——. A Letter from the Army. 1647.

——. A New Quaere, at This Time Seasonably to Be Considered. 1646. Contained in Some Drops of the Viall. 1646.

——. The Opening of Master Prynnes New Book. 1646. Contained in Some Drops of the Viall. 1646.

——. A Peace But No Pacification: or, an Answer to That New Designe of the Oath of Pacification and Accommodation. 1643.

——. The Practice of Policie in a Christian Life. 1639.

——. Reasons for Unitie, Peace, and Love. 1646. Contained in Some Drops of the Viall. 1646.

——. The Smoke in the Temple. 3d ed. 1646. Contained in Some Drops of the Viall. 1646.

——. A Solemn Discourse upon the Sacred League and Covenant of Both Kingdomes, Opening the Divinity and Policy of It. 1644.

——. Sparkles of Glory, or, Some Beams of the Morning-Star. 1647.

——. Sparkles of Glory, or Some Beams of the Morning-Star. 1847 edition.

——. A Voice from Heaven. 1644.

[——]. Wonderfull Predictions Declared in a Message, as from the Lord. 1648.

Schenk, Wilhelm. The Concern for Social Justice in the Puritan Revolution. 1948.

——. "A Democratic Tercentenary," *The Hibbert Journal,* XLVI (1947), 69–74.

————. "The Religion of the Spirit in Seventeenth-Century England," *Church Quarterly Review*, CXL (1945), 12–28.

Schlatter, Richard. B. "The Higher Learning in Puritan England," *Historical Magazine of the Protestant Episcopal Church*, XXIII (1954), 167–87.

Schlatter, Richard, ed. Richard Baxter and Puritan Politics. New Brunswick, N.J., 1957.

[Sedgwick, William], Animadversions upon a Letter and Paper, First Sent to His Highness by Certain Gentlemen and Others in Wales. N.p., 1656.

————. Justice upon the Armie Remonstrance. 1649.

————. The Leaves of the Tree of Life: for the Healing of the Nations. 1648.

————. Mr. William Sedgwicks Letter to His Excellency Thomas Lord Fairfax. N.p., 1649.

————. Scripture a Perfect Rule for Church-Government. 1643.

————. A Second View of the Army Remonstrance. 1649.

————. Some Flashes of Lightnings of the Sonne of Man. 1648.

————. The Spirituall Madman, or a Prophesie Concerning, the King, the Parliament, London, the Army. N.p., 1648.

————. Zions Deliverance and Her Friends Duty. 2d ed. 1643.

Shaw, William A. A History of the English Church During the Civil Wars and Under the Commonwealth, 1640–1660. 2 vols. 1900.

Sibthorp, Robert. Apostolike Obedience. 1627.

Simpson, Alan. Puritanism in Old and New England. Chicago, 1955.

Sippell, Theodor. Werdendes Quäkertum. Stuttgart, 1937.

————. William Dells Programm einer "lutherischen" Gemeinschaftsbewegung. Tübingen, 1911.

Smith, Goldwin. "The Reform of the Laws of England, 1640–1660," *University of Toronto Quarterly*, X (1941), 469–81.

Solt, Leo F. "Anti-Intellectualism in the Puritan Revolution," *Church History*, XXV (1956), 306–16.

————. "John Saltmarsh: New Model Army Chaplain," *The Journal of Ecclesiastical History*, II (1951), 69–80.

————. "What Was Cromwell's Religion?" *The Listener*, LX (4 September 1958), 335–36.

————. "William Dell: New Model Army Chaplain," *Church Quarterly Review*, CLV (1954), 43–55.

Sprigge, Joshua. Anglia Rediviva: England's Recovery. New ed. Oxford, 1854.

———. Christus Redivivus. 1649.

———. A Further Testimony to the Glory That Is Near. 1649.

———. Solace for Saints in the Saddest Times. 1648.

———. A Testimony to an Approaching Glory. 1648.

Stearns, Raymond Phineas. Congregationalism in the Dutch Netherlands. Studies in Church History, Vol. IV. Chicago: The American Society of Church History. 1940.

———. The Strenuous Puritan, Hugh Peter, 1598–1660. Urbana, Ill., 1954.

Stearns, Raymond Phineas, ed. "Letters and Documents by or Relating to Hugh Peter," *The Essex Institute Historical Collections*, LXXI (1935), 303–18; LXXII (1936), 43–72, 117–34, 208–32, 303–49; LXXIII (1937), 130–57.

Stumpf, Samuel Enoch. Democracy and The Christian Faith. Nashville, Tenn., 1950.

Tanner, J. R. English Constitutional Conflicts of the Seventeenth Century, 1603–1689. Cambridge, England, 1928.

Tanner, J. R., ed. Constitutional Documents of the Reign of James I. Cambridge, England, 1930.

Tawney, R. H. Religion and the Rise of Capitalism. Mentor Books Edition. New York, 1947.

Thirteen Strange Prophesies. [1648].

XXXII Propositions or Articles Subscribed by Severall Reformed Churches. 1647.

Trevor-Roper, H. R. Historical Essays. 1957.

Trinterud, Leonard J. "The Origins of Puritanism," *Church History*, XX (1951), 37–57.

Troeltsch, Ernest. The Social Teaching of the Christian Churches. Translated by Olive Wyon. 2 vols. 1931.

The True Informer. 5–12 July 1645.

Twelve Strange Prophesies. N.p., n.d.

Two Letters Sent to the Honoble William Lenthal Esq. 1645.

Tyndall, William Y. John Bunyan, Mechanik Preacher. New York, 1934.

Umfreville, William. An Information for Mr. William Dell the (Right Reformer) As He Is Pleased to Stile Himself. 1646.

Vaughan, Rice. A Plea for the Common-Laws of England. 1651.
Venn, John, and John Archibald Venn, eds. Alumni Canta-
brigienses. 4 vols. Cambridge, England, 1922–27.
Vicars, John. The Burning-Bush Not Consumed. 1646.
Vincent, W. A. L. The State and School Education, 1640–1660,
in England and Wales. 1950.

Walker, Clement. The Compleat History of Independency
upon the Parliament begun 1640. 1661.
[William Walwyn]. The Power of Love. 1643.
———. A Whisper in the Eare of Mr. Thomas Edwards. 1646.
[Ward, Nathaniel]. A Word to Mr. Peters, and Two Words for
the Parliament and Kingdom. 1647.
[Ward, Seth]. Vindiciae Academiarum. Oxford, 1654.
Weber, Max. The Protestant Ethic and the Spirit of Capitalism.
Translated by Talcott Parsons. 1930.
Webster, John. Academiarum Examen, or the Examination of
Academies. 1654.
———. The Judgement Set, and the Bookes Opened. 1654.
———. The Saints Guide, or, Christ the Rule, and Ruler of
Saints. 1654.
Whitelock, Bulstrode. Memorials of the English Affairs. New
ed. 4 vols. Oxford, 1853.
Whitfield, Thomas. A Refutation of the Loose Opinions, and
Licentious Tenets. 1646.
Williams, David. A History of Modern Wales. 1950.
Williams, Roger. The Bloudy Tenent of Persecution for Cause
of Conscience Discussed: and Mr. Cotton's Letter Examined
and Answered. Edited by Edward Bean Underhill. Hanserd
Knollys Society. 1848.
———. Publications of the Narragansett Club. First series. Sub-
scribers' edition. 6 vols. Providence, R.I., 1866–74.
Winstanley, Gerrard. The Works of Gerrard Winstanley. Ed-
ited by George H. Sabine. Ithaca, N.Y., 1941.
Wolfe, Don M. Milton and the Puritan Revolution. New York,
1941.
Wolfe, Don M., ed. Leveller Manifestoes of the Puritan Revolution. New York, 1944.
Wood, Anthony à. Athenae Oxonienses. Edited by Philip Bliss.
4 vols. 1813–20.

Woodhouse, A. S. P. "Background for Milton," *University of Toronto Quarterly,* X (1941), 499–505.

——. "Milton, Puritanism, and Liberty," *University of Toronto Quarterly,* IV (1935), 483–513.

——. "Puritanism and Liberty," *University of Toronto Quarterly,* IV (1935), 395–403.

——. Puritanism and Liberty, Being the Army Debates (1647–9) from the Clarke Manuscripts with Supplementary Documents. 2d ed. Chicago, 1951.

——. "Religion and Some Foundations of English Democracy," *Philosophical Review,* LXI (1952), 503–31.

Works of Darkness Brought to Light. 1647.

Wormuth, Francis D. The Origins of Modern Constitutionalism. New York, 1949.

——. The Royal Prerogative, 1603–1649. Ithaca, N.Y., 1939.

Wortley, Francis. Characters and Elegies. N.p., 1646.

Wright, Louis B. Middle-Class Culture in Elizabethan England. Chapel Hill, N.C., 1935.

Yule, George. The Independents in the English Civil War. Cambridge, England, 1958.

Zagorin, Perez. A History of Political Thought in the English Revolution. 1954.

Index